Cambridge Elements ≡

Elements in Publishing and Book Culture
edited by
Samantha Rayner
University College London
Rebecca Lyons
University of Bristol

BOOK CLUBS AND BOOK COMMERCE

Corinna Norrick-Rühl

Johannes Gutenberg University Mainz

This title is also available as Open Access on Cambridge Core.

CAMBRIDGE
UNIVERSITY PRESS

CAMBRIDGE
UNIVERSITY PRESS

University Printing House, Cambridge CB2 8BS, United Kingdom

One Liberty Plaza, 20th Floor, New York, NY 10006, USA

477 Williamstown Road, Port Melbourne, VIC 3207, Australia

314–321, 3rd Floor, Plot 3, Splendor Forum, Jasola District Centre,
New Delhi – 110025, India

79 Anson Road, #06–04/06, Singapore 079906

Cambridge University Press is part of the University of Cambridge.

It furthers the University's mission by disseminating knowledge in the pursuit of
education, learning, and research at the highest international levels of excellence.

www.cambridge.org
Information on this title: www.cambridge.org/9781108708814
DOI: 10.1017/9781108597258

© Corinna Norrick-Rühl 2019

First published 2019

A catalog record for this publication is available from the British Library.

ISBN 978-1-108-70881-4 Paperback
ISSN 2514-8524 (online)
ISSN 2514-8516 (print)

Book Clubs and Book Commerce

Elements in Publishing and Book Culture

DOI: 10.1017/9781108597258

First published: December 2019

Corinna Norrick-Rühl

Johannes Gutenberg University Mainz

Author for correspondence: Corinna Norrick-Rühl norrick@uni-mainz.de

ABSTRACT: In the twentieth century, cumulative millions of readers received books by mail from clubs like the Book-of-the-Month Club, the Book Society or Bertelsmann Club. This Element offers an introduction to book clubs as a distribution channel and cultural phenomenon and shows that book clubs and book commerce are linked inextricably. It argues that a global perspective is necessary to understand the cultural and economic impact of book clubs in the twentieth and into the twenty-first centuries. It also explores central reasons for book club membership, condensing them into four succinct categories: convenience, community, concession and most importantly curation.

This title is also available as Open Access on Cambridge Core.

KEYWORDS: book sales clubs, book distribution, book clubs, mail-order book culture, book ownership

ISBNs: 9781108708814 (PB), 9781108597258 (OC)

ISSNs: 2514-8524 (online), 2514-8516 (print)

Contents

1 Introduction

In 1943, the cartoonist Helen E. Hokinson (1893–1949),[1] known for her anthropological eye for society and culture, published a vignette about the Book-of-the-Month Club (BOMC) in the *New Yorker* magazine. One of Hokinson's famous ladies, with their plump form, small feet and friendly faces, says to her hometown librarian, "I'm afraid this is goodbye, Miss MacDonald. I'm joining the Book-of-the-Month Club."[2] In this cartoon, a subscription to a book sales club relieves the reader of the need for recommendations from and conversations with the librarian (many of whom were portrayed by Hokinson over the years) and of the necessity to use the library infrastructure. Instead, the reader now waits at home for the monthly delivery – looking forward to the missive from the book club, which will not only include a book but also an extensive review by a member of the club's editorial board – an idea which the *New York Times* touted "Harry Scherman's best SOFT-SELL IDEA" (see also Section 3).[3] In an ironic twist, the cartoon was used in BOMC ads once a year.[4]

In 1944, Hokinson's protagonist from the 1943 cartoon is sitting on her couch, decked out in heels and pearls, with a friend, who is equally well groomed. She has waited patiently for her Book-of-the-Month to arrive and is now opening her parcel. Anachronistically speaking, she is "unboxing"[5] her Book-of-the-Month. As she unboxes the book, she says, "What I like

---

[1] R. C. Harvey, "Helen E. Hokinson," *The Comics Journal* (July 22, 2013), www.tcj.com/helen-e-hokinson/.

[2] H. E. Hokinson, "I'm afraid this is goodbye" [cartoon], *New Yorker*, XIX (Nov. 13, 1943), 39, 105.

[3] W. Glaberson, "The Book Clubs, Chapter 2," *New York Times* (July 12, 1987), 153.

[4] Cf. E. Fitzgerald, *A Nickel an Inch. A Memoir* (New York: Atheneum, 1985), p. 267.

[5] *Urban Dictionary* definition: "The Internet trend of showing photos or video from the unpacking of a retail box of some desirable product, such as the latest laptop or portable music player." 2GooD, "Unboxing" in *Urban Dictionary* (Feb. 1, 2008), www.urbandictionary.com/define.php?term=unboxing. For more detail, cf. R. Noorda, "The Element of Surprise: A Study of Children's Book Subscription Boxes in the USA," *Publishing Research Quarterly*, 35 (2019) 2, 223–35, 227–8.

about the Book-of-the-Month Club is the <u>suspense</u>."[6] Since the cartoon is a stand-alone vignette, we are left to wonder: Does she like the suspense of not knowing which book will be sent to her? Or does she think the books themselves are filled with suspense? Or is it a combination of the two: the anticipation and the reading pleasure?

These two cartoons emphasize a number of issues surrounding book sales clubs that make them so relevant to book and publishing historians, historians of reading and literature, and cultural sociologists – to name a few of the fields that can profit from a deeper understanding of the workings and intricacies of book sales clubs in the twentieth and twenty-first centuries.

Book sales clubs, also referred to as publisher book clubs, offer an interesting vantage point from which to observe the book trade, since they are a well-established and long-standing distribution channel and have evolved over time to adapt to different market requirements. As institutions within the literary marketplace, they contribute to the negotiation of values and practices associated with reading. In addition, their history (mergers, closures, restructuring, relaunches, etc.) can help us understand the challenges the book industry is facing more generally.

This Element will offer a comprehensive analysis of the significance of book clubs in relation to the book industry, answering overarching questions about the structures, members, and appeal of the book club. Existing studies tend to focus on the local or national context. However, already in 1938, at a meeting of English P.E.N., participants discussed the effects of book clubs as a "development which was not restricted by national boundaries."[7] Their observations were true: book clubs are central to the global history of the book, not least through their significance for the foundation and spread of international media conglomerates. I will argue that patterns in the history of book clubs are similar across national boundaries and markets and show how the book club business was intertwined internationally. Given the limits of the Element format, I will mainly focus on examples from the British, German, and US book industries. This

---

[6] H. E. Hokinson, "What I like about the Book-of-the-Month Club . . . " [cartoon], *New Yorker*, XX (July 29, 1944) 24, 57. Underline in the original.

[7] See also "Book Societies and Effect on Shops," *Times* (Jan. 5, 1938), 12.

choice was motivated by source availability and by the fact that these three nations' book industries have consistently been three of the most active and profitable worldwide throughout the twentieth and into the twenty-first centuries.[8] Whenever possible, I will also draw on other book industry data to illustrate international trends and transnational similarities. When quotes are translated into English, the translations are my own.

Section 2 will outline the economics of the book club distribution model in relation to different book industry players. It will also discuss the cultural impact of book clubs and the theoretical frameworks for analysis and comparison of book clubs. Section 2 will conclude with the introduction of a model (the four Cs) to further structure our understanding of book clubs.

Then, Section 3 will focus on book clubs in the twentieth century. We will see which companies shaped our understanding of the clubs – and how they have contributed to the international publishing landscape through their driving role in the foundation and expansion of (inter-)national multimedia conglomerates such as Bertelsmann and Holtzbrinck. We will also consider how the book clubs reacted to fundamental changes in the book industry landscape such as the introduction of big box bookstores and bookstore chains and the rise of internet bookselling. We will explore forms of membership and see how members' magazines or newsletters and other corporate publishing outputs contribute(d) to the establishment of a certain image for each individual publisher book club. In addition, the research points toward the role book design and – more broadly speaking – paratexts[9] and marketing of the book as a collectible object play(ed) in the heyday of the book clubs and beyond. Section 4 will consider chances and challenges for book clubs today in the face of an increasingly digital literary

---

[8] The WIPO-IPA report on *The Global Publishing Industry in 2016* ranked the United States first for total revenue from sales and licensing for the retail sector, Germany third, and the UK fifth. Cf. WIPO/IPA, *The Global Publishing Industry in 2016*, [Geneva] 2018. www.wipo.int/edocs/pubdocs/en/wipo_i pa_pilotsurvey_2016.pdf, p. 7 (table 1).

[9] Cf. G. Genette, *Paratexts. Thresholds of Interpretation* (Cambridge: Cambridge University Press, 1997).

sphere,[10] drawing on best practice examples that are still active today. Section 5 will offer some conclusions and an outlook.

A multi-method approach was employed to grasp the complex history and present state of the book club. This Element builds on countless individual histories of book clubs. Archival research and interviews supplemented the existing studies. The digital archives of the *New York Times* and the *London Times* have proven to be a treasure trove for insights on the history of the book club business in the Anglophone world and beyond. Other sources for this study included but were not limited to archival materials from Mainzer Verlagsarchiv and the Special Collections at Universiteit van Amsterdam; the online catalogs of the British Library, Deutsche Nationalbiblothek and the Library of Congress; the digital archives of *LIFE*, *New Yorker*, *Spiegel* and *Zeit*; selected club members' magazines available to the author at time of writing; and a small set of semi-structured interviews[11] with employees and former employees of German book clubs.

2 Book Clubs: Definition and Basic Structures

When Joseph W. Kappel wrote about the influence of club selections on the evaluation of books in 1948, he began by "describ[ing] briefly how book clubs operate" and quickly admitted that this "is by no means a simple task."[12] This section will attempt to sketch out the basics of book clubs. After a brief disambiguation of the term "book club" and observations on the inconspicuousness of book clubs in book historical models and research, Section 2.1 will discuss the main types of book clubs. Section 2.2 will then consider the basic economic ideas that drive publisher book clubs, followed by Section 2.3, which will foreground the cultural impact of the clubs.

[10] Cf. S. Murray, "Charting the Digital Literary Sphere," *Contemporary Literature*, 56 (2015), 2, 311–39.

[11] Cf. C. Hopf, "Qualitative Interviews – ein Überblick" in U. Flick, et al. (eds.), *Qualitative Forschung. Ein Handbuch*, 8th edn. (Reinbek: Rowohlt, 2010), pp. 349–60.

[12] J. W. Kappel, "Book Clubs and Evaluations of Books," *Public Opinion Quarterly* 12 (1948), 2, 243–52, 244.

It is first useful to disambiguate the term "book club." While other languages (such as Dutch, French and German) differentiate between book discussion clubs (Dutch: *leesclub, leeskring*; French: *club de lecture, cercle de lecture*; German: *Lesekreis, Literaturkreis*), bibliophile book clubs (Dutch: *bibliofielenclub*; French: *société bibliophile, société des bibliophiles;* German: *Bibliophilenverein, Bibliophilengesellschaft*) and book sales clubs (Dutch: *boekenclub*; French: *club de livres*; German: *Buchgemeinschaft*), the English term "book clubs" can lead to misinterpretations.[13] There are at least four established meanings of the term from an Anglophone point of view, some of which are used in overlapping ways:

1. Firstly, and most importantly for our context here, the term "book clubs" can be used to denote "book-distribution institutions"[14] that offer(ed) an alternative to traditional book buying in bricks-and-mortar bookstores. These commercial organizations worked as distributors if they bought in published books and resold them below retail price. They could also work as publisher-distributors if they (a) bought in licenses for published books and published their own, rebadged editions or (b) published their own list of original editions or new, special editions of already published material.

   The book clubs sold their products via a subscription model (club membership), often at a substantial discount, which is why they are sometimes known as discount book clubs. Other terms used are book sales clubs, commercial book clubs, direct-to-consumer book clubs, publisher book clubs or sometimes even publishing book clubs.

Unless otherwise stated, in this Element, "book club" will refer to the first meaning detailed here. These other meanings are also in use:

2. Book clubs, also known as book discussion clubs, reading groups, book groups or literature circles, include 'small, peer-led discussion groups

---

[13] I am grateful to C. Krömer (Le Mans) and L. Kuitert (Amsterdam) for assistance in verifying translations of these terms.

[14] J. Harker, *America the Middlebrow. Women's Novels, Progressivism, and Middlebrow Authorship between the Wars* (Amherst/Boston: University of Massachusetts Press, 2007), p. 16.

whose members have chosen to read the same story, poem, article, or book. ... Each group follows a reading and meeting schedule, holding periodic discussions on the way through the book."[15] Today, this is the most common use of the term.[16] These book discussion clubs have received much scholarly[17] and media attention – even before, but especially after, TV celebrity Oprah Winfrey founded Oprah's Book Club.[18]

3. Sometimes the term "book club" describes bibliophile societies such as the Caxton Club in Chicago or the Book Club of California, which can be "bodies formed for the printing of works which would not, because of their specialized nature, be published as commercial ventures."[19] Elsewhere, the term "book collectors clubs"[20] is employed.

4. In her oft-quoted thesis *Fiction and the Reading Public*, Q. D. Leavis uses the term "book-club" when referring to subscription library structures and/or literary societies in the eighteenth and nineteenth centuries, directly quoting from nineteenth-century sources about a "Country Book-Club."[21] In clubs and societies such as these, members had access to libraries, that is, for borrowing books or for reading them on club premises. Leavis also writes in an explicitly derogatory way about the

---

[15] H. Daniels, *Literature Circle: Voice and Choice in Book Clubs and Reading Groups*, 2nd edn. (Portsmouth, NH: Stenhouse Publishers, 2002), p. 2.

[16] Cf. G. Clark and A. Phillips, *Inside Book Publishing*, 5th edn. (Abingdon: Routledge, 2014), p. 296.

[17] For more context, cf. E. Long, *Book Clubs: Women and the Uses of Reading in Everyday Life* (Chicago: University of Chicago Press, 2003).

[18] For more context, cf. for instance chap. 4 in T. Striphas, *The Late Age of Print. Everyday Book Culture from Consumerism to Control* (New York: Columbia University Press, 2009) or C. K. Farr, *Reading Oprah* (Albany: State University of New York Press, 2004).

[19] G. A. Glaister, *Encyclopedia of the Book*, 2nd edn. (New Castle, DE: Oak Knoll Press, 1996), p. 62.

[20] S. E. Berger, *The Dictionary of the Book. A Glossary for Book Collectors, Booksellers, Librarians, and Others* (Lanham: Rowman & Littlefield, 2016), p. 34.

[21] Q. D. Leavis, *Fiction and the Reading Public* (Harmondsmouth: Penguin, 1979), pp. 111, 123–5.

first modern book sales club in Britain, the Book Society (established in 1929 in the UK, discontinued in 1969) but does not employ the term "club" in this context.[22]

Besides the ambiguity of the term "book club," there is an additional challenge when working with book industry data. Some studies conflate book clubs as a sales channel with "direct sales" and "mail order"; in other studies, the difference between "direct sales," "mail order" and "book clubs" is pronounced. This affects the comparability of the statistics, though the conflation of the categories bears witness to the manifold activities of the clubs, which sold products to their members door-to-door, through mail-order catalogs, book club buses, shop-in-shop models, or dedicated club bookstores and later the internet.

Book clubs as book-distribution institutions have a long and varied (and international) history. However, book-distribution institutions seem to suffer from academic neglect. Madeleine B. Stern observed, "In the card and directory catalog of the New York Public Library, there is nothing that stands between the listings BOOKS-DISINFECTION and BOOKS-DUMMIES. The ... entries[] BOOKS-DISSEMINATION and BOOKS-DISTRIBUTION are conspicuous by their absence."[23] Monika Estermann argues similarly, emphasizing that scholarly examinations of book distributors are extremely rare compared to publishing and publishers' histories or corporate histories and commemorative volumes for publishers.[24] While the journal *Book History* has published a number of articles on the state of the

---

[22] Cf. N. Wilson, "Middlemen, Middlebrow, Broadbrow," in C. Ferrall and D. McNeill (eds.), *British Literature in Transition, 1920–1940: Futility and Anarchy* (Cambridge: Cambridge University Press, 2018), pp. 315–30 (passim).

[23] M. B. Stern, "Dissemination of Popular Books in the Midwest and Far West during the Nineteenth Century," in M. Hackenberg (ed.), *Getting the Books Out. Papers of the Chicago Conference on the Book in 19th-Century America* (Honolulu: University Press of the Pacific, 2005), pp. 76–97, 76.

[24] M. Estermann, "Buchhandel, Buchhandelsgeschichte und Verlagsgeschichts-schreibung vom 18. Jahrhundert bis zur Gegenwart," in U. Rautenberg (ed.), *Buchwissenschaft in Deutschland* (Berlin/Boston: de Gruyter Saur, 2013), pp. 257–320, 304.

discipline for a variety of topics (reading, online reading, textbooks, history of archives, etc.), questions of bookselling and distribution have not been highlighted in this way. Distributors are certainly underrepresented in book trade and publishing history studies, although they figure as equally important actors in the standard book historical models we refer to, such as Darnton's communications circuit (1982) or Adams/Barker's "New Model for the Study of the Book" (1993).[25] The imbalance has various reasons. As precarious as their situation may be, publishers' archives are better preserved and more easily available than sources relating to distributors and distribution.[26] However, there has recently been a welcome surge in interest in bookselling and distribution questions, and this seems to be a growing area.[27]

Book clubs as a specific entity are all but missing from the models we rely on in the first instance as book historians: simply put, Darnton's observations take their starting point in examples from the eighteenth century, meaning an inclusion of the twentieth-century book club model would have been more than anachronistic. While he could have included subscription, he does not, though he does include clubs as an option for readers, giving early literary circles and societies a nod. In general, however, the one-way circuitry of the model does not allow for direct sales methods, because these would have to cross through the middle of the circuit and connect publisher and reader (buyer) directly. While Adams and Barker omit book clubs in their model, the omission goes hand in hand with a more general focus on structures, and less on actors and institutions. In the

[25] R. Darnton, "What Is the History of Books?" *Daedalus*, 111 (1982), 3, 65–83; T. Adams/N. Barker, "A New Model for the Study of the Book," in D. Finkelstein and A. McCleery (eds.), *The Book History Reader*, 2nd edn. (Abingdon: Routledge, 2006), pp. 47–65.

[26] Regarding the availability of publisher archives, cf. for instance D. Gastell, "Verlagsgeschichtsschreibung ohne Verlagsarchiv," in C. Norrick and U. Schneider (eds.), *Verlagsgeschichtsschreibung. Modelle und Archivfunde* (Wiesbaden: Harrassowitz, 2012), pp. 46–59.

[27] As evidenced by discussions at SHARP 2019, e.g., during Panel 3.6. Some of these discussions were continued on the conference hashtag #sharp19.

Adams/Barker model, book clubs could be categorized as belonging to either "publication," "manufacture" or "distribution," since the structures and models can fulfill any of those three category briefs. We can assume that the two bibliographers would agree, since they understood their reaction to Darnton's model as a way to map relationships between organizations and processes, rather than static positions of actors in a circuit. Finally, the late-twentieth-century print publishing communications circuit developed by Padmini Ray Murray and Claire Squires also omits book clubs, though they could have possibly been included in their category "Wholesalers and Distributors." In contrast, Ray Murray and Squires name "subscriber" as a possible role for twenty-first-century readers in their "Digital Publishing Communications Circuit."[28]

2.1 Book Club Basics

When dealing with books, which are simultaneously commodities and cultural objects, it can be difficult to divorce the economic from the cultural perspective. The two perspectives are intertwined. German-language scholars and book industry specialists alike use the term "double character of the book" to denote this interconnection.[29] This double character applies to book clubs, too. The different options to break down book sales clubs into subcategories lean to either the cultural or the economic perspective.

If we favor a cultural perspective, we can categorize book clubs according to their lists. We can consider the list through distant reading and statistical analysis of the catalog. On the one hand, we could compare depth – availability of options in a particular field/genre. On the other hand, we could compare breadth – availability of diverse options covering a spectrum of fields/genres. A cultural-leaning focus could look at the

---

[28] P. Ray Murray and C. Squires, "The Digital Publishing Communications Circuit," *Book 2.0*, 3 (2013), 1, 3–23.

[29] "Doppelcharakter des Buches." Cf., e.g., H. Volpers, "Der internationale Buchmarkt," in J.-F. Leonhard, et al. (eds.), *Medienwissenschaft: Ein Handbuch zur Entwicklung der Medien und Kommunikationsformen. 3. Teilband* (Berlin/New York: de Gruyter, 2002), pp. 2649–60, 2649.

materiality of the book club editions and discuss their status as cultural signifiers (cf. Section 2.4).

If we lean towards the economic perspective, we can categorize book clubs by their corporate status. Just as John B. Thompson suggests for publishers in his monograph *Merchants of Culture*, we can situate the different companies on a continuum, from independent to corporate ownership.[30] As we will see, many clubs started out independently and were taken over by the big conglomerate players like Doubleday, Time Warner or Bertelsmann. Others were founded as part of conglomerate growth strategies.

We can also classify book clubs by their point of sale, that is, whether they sell via mail-order catalog, employing door-to-door salespeople, in dedicated bricks-and-mortar book club retail sites or in shop-in-shop retail sites. As will be described in the historical overview, many clubs chose to offer their members a combination of these sales strategies to maximize reach and visibility, as well as for brand building and recruitment.

According to Weissbach, however, all of these categories – whether informed by a cultural or economic perspective – are not specific to book clubs.[31] The categories are also applicable to any publisher. Weissbach argues that we can differentiate clubs in the most straightforward way by looking at the membership requirements and the relationship between the consumers and the club. Here, Weissbach distinguishes between clubs with a direct subscription of specific titles of a series or collection and clubs with a membership fee structure.

For Germany, examples of the former are the Bibliothek der Unterhaltung und des Wissens or Welt im Buch. These clubs with a direct subscription of specific titles were especially prevalent in the early history of the clubs, before World War II. However, it became clear that to retain members, clubs needed to offer selection options and more flexibility.

[30] J. B. Thompson, *Merchants of Culture. The Publishing Business in the Twenty-First Century*, 2nd edn. (New York: Plume, 2012), p. 129.

[31] F. Weissbach, "Buchgemeinschaften als Vertriebsform im Buchhandel," in *Buchgemeinschaften in Deutschland* (Hamburg: Verlag für Buchmarkt-Forschung, 1969), pp. 17–101, 54.

Thus, most clubs founded later in the century operated or transitioned into the second type of club, the type with a membership fee structure. The membership fee is (or was) due monthly, quarterly or annually. In turn, members choose (or chose) a book on a regular, contractual basis.

Within this type of club, there were different options. Some book clubs established the marketing technique known as "negative option": "automatically shipping goods unless customers instructed them not to."[32] This condition of membership relied "heavily on the lethargy of the member in returning his refusal on time,"[33] that is, on the so-called inertia factor[34] and was very successful for the better part of the twentieth century. Other clubs worked with a "positive option" (analogously, though the term is not well established). That is, they either offered their members a free choice from a catalog, whereby the book needed to have a certain monetary value, or – and this is the most flexible option for consumers – required members to buy one book of any value on a regular, contractual basis.

2.2 Economics of Book Clubs

The economic framework that forms the basis for the book club business consists of three elements: (a) direct-mail selling and marketing, (b) infrastructural advantages, and (c) benefits of scale.

Direct mail selling is "a form of direct marketing in which sales literature or other promotional material is mailed directly to selected potential purchasers."[35] Mail-order shopping is the most important historical

---

[32] J. S. Rubin, "The Book-of-the-Month Club," in P. S. Boyer (ed.), *The Oxford Companion to United States History* (Oxford: Oxford University Press, 2004), www.oxfordreference.com/view/10.1093/acref/9780195082098.001.0001/acref-9780195082098-e-0191.

[33] L. Shatzkin, *In Cold Type: Overcoming the Book Crisis* (Boston: Houghton Mifflin, 1983), p. 32.

[34] D. Bonner, *Revolutionizing Children's Records. The Young People's Records and Children's Record Guild Series, 1946–1977* (Lanham: Scarecrow Press, 2008), p. 20.

[35] See also "direct marketing" in J. Law (ed.), *A Dictionary of Business and Management*, 6th edn. (Oxford: Oxford University Press, 2016), www.oxfordreference.com/view/10.1093/acref/9780199684984.001.0001/acref-9780199684984-e-3873#.

precursor for the book club business, emerging in both Europe and North America at the end of the nineteenth century. Early mail-order houses such as Montgomery Ward and Sears in the United States paved the way for an entirely new and convenient form of consumer behavior. From the late nineteenth century on, catalogs became "a perennially popular selling tool."[36] Beginning with individual sheets listing goods, soon the catalogs, filled with photographs and sometimes called wish books,[37] "served not only as a marketing tool, but also as school readers, almanacs, symbols of abundance and progress, and objects of fantasy and desire."[38] Ellen D. Gilbert emphasizes in the *Oxford Companion to the Book* that "regardless of what country or market [they] serve[]," mail-order businesses "always depended upon a reliable delivery system."[39] This was the case in both Europe and North America by the beginning of the twentieth century, thus paving the way for the success of mail-order book culture.

A major difference to bricks-and-mortar sales was the fact that mail-order houses did not have to rent and staff retail premises. The mail-order houses could pass these savings on to the customers as competitive prices, undercutting store retailers.

Risk factors of direct mail selling, however, include a lack of continuity and an impersonal relationship between the retailer and customer. Millions of catalogs were mailed to customers who had no obligation to buy the products depicted. Mail order is still ubiquitous, though on the decline. In 2007, a peak year, 19.62 billion catalogs were mailed to American

[36] J. Appelbaum, "Paperback Talk. Sales Through the Mails," *New York Times Book Review* (Nov. 28, 1982), 31–2, 31.

[37] In the case of books, this term conflated the catalog with the product. See also, "Mail order" in J. M. Woodham (ed.), *A Dictionary of Modern Design* (Oxford: Oxford University Press, 2016), www.oxfordreference.com/view/10.1093/acref/9780191762963.001.0001/acref-9780191762963-e-521.

[38] M. R. Wilson, "Mail Order," in J. R. Grossmann (ed.), *The Encyclopedia of Chicago* (Chicago: University of Chicago Press, 2004), pp. 505–6, 505.

[39] E. D. Gilbert, "Mail-order Catalog," in M. F. Suarez and S. J. and H. R. Woodhuysen (eds.), *Oxford Companion to the Book* (Oxford: Oxford University Press, 2010), vol. 2, pp. 907–8.

households.[40] Some risk factors associated with direct mail selling were alleviated by the membership structures of book clubs. Through the membership system, "continuity marketing" was possible – that is, marketing to an existing customer base which had already made an initial purchase.[41] The principles of direct mail selling and continuity marketing were further combined with a contractual minimum purchase or membership fee, which guaranteed regular income and thus liquidity for the club.

For the members, certain types of advertising could be reframed and expanded to create a sense of belonging and community, thus counteracting the potential anonymity of mail order. An example is the expansion of the traditional catalog into what Vera Dumont calls "magalogs." Catalogs were the central method of communication with the membership for the clubs. Dumont chooses the term "magalog" to describe a blend between magazines and catalogs.[42] Although the book club employees in the semi-structured interviews did not use this term, they confirmed the dual function of the book club missives. According to Dumont, magalogs fulfilled two functions. First, they conveniently informed the members about main and possibly alternate selections (other books available to the members, which counted toward their contractual quota of books per quarter or year) as well as other offers and discounts. The magalog reached the members within the comfort of their own homes and simultaneously encouraged them to recruit new members. Second, the catalogs also took on the functions of bulletins, newsletters or magazines, including editorial content that was an added bonus for members. By offering their members a monthly or quarterly magalog, the club emphasized the community element of belonging to the club and downplayed the commodification of the books by embedding the selections in a larger editorial context with "author interviews, excerpts

---

[40] DMA, "Number of catalogs mailed in the United States from 2001 to 2015 (in billions)," *Statista* (2019), www.statista.com/statistics/735150/catalogs-mailed-usa/.

[41] Cf. Bonner, *Revolutionizing Children's Records*, p. 17.

[42] V. Dumont, "Literatur- und Buchvermittlung an ein Millionenpublikum. Charakteristika der Literatur- und Buchdiskurse in den Mitgliederzeitschriften der Büchergilde Gutenberg und des Bertelsmann-Leserings in den 1950er Jahren," *Gutenberg-Jahrbuch*, 92 (2017), 181–200, 182.

from books" as well as "guest editors and contributors."[43] The clubs also contributed significantly to the creation of paratexts – epitexts, to be precise – with these publications. Compared to epitexts in highbrow literary or intellectual outlets, these epitexts were widely read and had a direct influence on commercial success of a book.

To use a marketing term anachronistically, these magalogs were early corporate publishing outputs. Though they incurred a significant cost (editorial, production, printing, mailing), magalogs were worth putting extra effort into, since the distribution loss was low: members had already expressed an interest in books and reading by joining the club, and thus, the advertising could be targeted to a greater extent than for regular mail-order enterprises. The magalogs had high circulation numbers and possibly a wider reach if members passed them along to neighbors and family.[44] Some were even available by subscription independent of membership, like *The Book Society News* (later: *The Bookman*);[45] Gollancz's *Left Book News* (later: *Left News*) was distributed gratis.[46] Furthermore, as Dumont argues convincingly, the club magalogs also shaped the popular image of reading and book ownership in social strata that may have had no other contact with the more traditional types of book talk in established media.[47] The club magalogs also, however, walked a fine line between culture and commerce: the BOMC described its publication, the *Book-of-the-Month Club News*, as a "literary magazine," which may be considered hyperbolic.[48] For many years, *The Book-of-the-Month Club News* featured famous paintings or reproductions of sculptures on the cover and information about the artwork

---

[43] M. Arnold, "Making Books. Book Clubs With a Mission," *New York Times* (Jan. 11, 2001), www.nytimes.com/2001/01/11/books/making-books-book-clubs-with-a-mission.html.

[44] M. Hutter and W. R. Langenbucher, *Buchgemeinschaften und Lesekultur* (Berlin: Spiess, 1980), p. 10.

[45] N. Wilson, "Broadbrows and Book Clubs," *British Academy Review* (2017), 29, 44–6, 44.

[46] Cf. I. Stevenson, *Book Makers* (London: British Library, 2010), p. 93.

[47] Dumont, "Literatur- und Buchvermittlung an ein Millionenpublikum," p.183.

[48] BOMC, "Give us your friends . . . " [advertisement] (1979).

and artist on the inside. Yet the painting or artwork had no bearing on the monthly selection or any other content of the magalog, creating an "odd dissonance" between the club's monthly choices and the displayed artwork.[49]

The impersonal relationship between the mail-order retailer and the consumer was a risk factor on the one hand, but an added bonus for other consumers. For people in rural areas, there was no option of having a relationship with a particular bookstore or bookseller. But for many people living in urban centers, there may have been the option to buy books in person, because there were bookstores or general and later department stores stocking books nearby. However, not every potential reader and book buyer might have felt comfortable doing so. Book clubs offered these people a certain element of independence – here, mail-order anonymity was ideal. In one word, these people may have exhibited what Germans called Schwellenangst, which is defined as the "fear of, or aversion to, crossing a threshold or entering a place, especially of a potential customer."[50] Especially for new or insecure readers, entering a bookstore was potentially daunting, because it meant holding one's own in a conversation with a knowledgeable and well-read salesperson.[51] The book clubs rendered Schwellenangst obsolete.

In a backward way, Schwellenangst may also have applied to customers who had access to a bookstore but did not want to discuss their reading preferences with their local booksellers or be seen buying certain genres. Ed Fitzgerald, president of Doubleday's book division and thus of the Literary Guild from 1960 to 1968, said that in the 1950s, the Literary Guild was

---

[49] J. Radway, *A Feeling for Books. The Book-of-the-Month Club, Literary Taste, and Middle-Class Desire* (Chapel Hill: University of North Carolina Press, 1997), p. 320.

[50] See also "Schwellenangst" in Yourdictionary.com, www.yourdictionary.com /schwellenangst.

[51] On the concept of "Schwellenangst," cf., e.g., M. Hutter and W. R. Langenbucher, *Buchgemeinschaften und Lesekultur*, p. 9 and M. Kollmannsberger, *Buchgemeinschaften im deutschen Buchmarkt: Funktionen, Leistungen, Wechselwirkungen* (Wiesbaden: Harrassowitz, 1995), pp. 89–92.

widely known as the "low-neckline club,"[52] with selections featuring "bloodless and deliberately titillating sex."[53] While he contributed to a change in the Literary Guild, rebranding it as the main rival of the BOMC and a club for general and literary fiction, the genre market still held sizable potential for book clubs throughout the second half of the twentieth century. For instance, in 2000, Doubleday Direct (owned by Bertelsmann) launched two genre book clubs in the same year, the first called Venus for "titles exploring sexual themes" and the second called Rhapsody, "featuring mass-market romance novels."[54]

Finally, from a marketing standpoint, mail-order marketing combined with a membership commitment enabled companies to conduct market research. Members' questionnaires and subscription databases were and are valuable sources for massing customer data, especially for clubs with high retention rates, where members remained loyal for years or even decades. Additional advertising could be targeted toward specific groups of members, for example, those more likely to buy non-fiction books.[55]

The infrastructural advantages that came from direct mail selling enabled book clubs to reach significantly more potential readers than the traditional sales channels of the book industry. Bookstores or other nonspecialized stores (general stores or later department stores) were the established go-between from publisher to reader. However, bookstores were more likely to be in urban, well-populated areas than in rural areas, and many potential readers at the beginning of the twentieth century simply did not have easy access to books and other consumer products. It is important to note that as Cooper, O'Connell, and Porter argue, home shopping of any kind had its "strongest appeal in areas of low consumer density." These were the areas "where the obvious price and distribution advantages available to mail-order companies as mass distributors were matched by the time-cost savings available to

---

[52] Fitzgerald, *A Nickel an Inch*, p. 145. [53] Ibid., p. 151.

[54] D. Carvajal, "Well-Known Book Clubs Agree to Form Partnership," *New York Times* (March 2, 2000), C2.

[55] For a concrete example, cf. S. Füssel, "The Bertelsmann Book Publishing Companies. 1945 to 2010," in *175 Years of Bertelsmann. The Legacy for Our Future* (Gütersloh: Bertelsmann, 2010), pp. 86–129, 104.

customers."[56] In 1946, John K. Hutchens wrote, "[e]ven those to whom the clubs are approximately anathema don't question the far-reaching effectiveness of the distribution system." He went on to share impressive distribution statistics: "of the 75,000 book packages mailed daily by the four Doubleday clubs, and the 15,000 by the Book-of-the-Month Club, [most] go to people in towns of less than 100,000 population." Furthermore, for the People's Book Club, "66 percent [we]re estimated to live in towns of less than 10,000, ten miles or more from the nearest book store. Thousands dwell in far places, on farms remote even from a village."[57] The mail-order business and the book clubs specifically were ideal business models for the United States after the establishment and implementation of Rural Free Delivery (RFD.) around the turn of the century. In 1929, Leon Whipple stated, "books are being made as accessible as milk on the stoop, ... as compulsory as spinach. ... Books are penetrating wherever the R.F.D. routes go."[58] Half of the US population lived in rural areas until as late as the 1920s. While book clubs may have been attractive for rural readers in other countries around the globe, in the British colonies in Africa or on the Indian subcontinent, some markets were not viable because they did not fulfill the prerequisites of a reliable postal system and delivery.

In the book club business, benefits of scale were impressive. Book historian Siegfried Lokatis wrote in a Festschrift for Bertelsmann in 2010 that to "outsiders vaguely familiar with the way publishers calculated the size of a print run in the pre-digital age, the economic machinations of a large book club seemed like a license to print money."[59] To break this

---

[56] R. Coopey, S. O'Connell, and D. Porter, "Mail Order in the United Kingdom c. 1880–1960: How Mail Order Competed with Other Forms of Retailing," *The International Review of Retail. Distribution and Consumer Research*, 3 (1999), 261–73, 264.

[57] J. K. Hutchens, "For Better or Worse, the Book Clubs. Their Organization, Aires, Methods and the Mass Market They Have Created," *New York Times Book Review* (March 31, 1946), 1, 24–8, 24.

[58] L. Whipple, "Books on the Belt," *The Nation*, 128 (Feb. 13, 1929), 3319, 182–3, 182.

[59] S. Lokatis, "A Concept Circles the Globe. From the Lesering to the Internationalization of the Club Business," in *175 Years of Bertelsmann*, pp. 132–71, 132.

down into more detail, we can use Thompson's different "benefits of scale." Thompson lists six benefits that large corporations have in the publishing sector: (1) rationalization of the back office, (2) dealing with suppliers, (3) negotiation with retailers, (4) advances, (5) ability to take risks (financial cushion), and (6) IT investment possibilities.[60] While not all of these benefits are applicable to book sales clubs – for instance, negotiation with retailers is irrelevant to direct sales – some are at least transferable.

Thompson's first and sixth points are certainly relevant to back office-heavy and IT-heavy mail-order enterprises. In fact, when Doubleday Direct (then owned by Bertelsmann) partnered with the BOMC (then owned by Time Warner) in 2000 (see Section 3.5) to form Bookspan, one of the main reasons was to combine "back office functions ... for profitability."[61]

Regarding Thompson's second point (dealing with suppliers), the type of suppliers dealt with depended on the book club's business model. For clubs buying rights to print a book club edition, suppliers were paper companies, printers, and so on. Book club print runs could be calculated more easily and precisely based on regular production cycles, subscriber numbers, and previous sales experiences. For book clubs buying the printed books in bulk from the original publisher, the original publishers themselves were the suppliers. Buying the books in bulk guaranteed low prime costs. Particularly in publishing, which is considered "a risky business" and where, more often than not, "successes subsidise the disappointments,"[62] the advantage of a stable membership base and easier calculation of print runs cannot be overstated. In 1948, average US publishers "beg[a]n to make profit on a book when sales approach[ed] 10,000." The BOMC, by comparison, at that point guaranteed "a publisher whose book is selected a minimum sale of 333,333 books . . . and the

---

[60] See Thompson, *Merchants of Culture*, pp. 147–52.

[61] S. Oda and G. Sanislo, *Book Publishing USA – Facts, Figures, Trends* (London: Holger Ehling 2001), p. 35.

[62] A. Franklin, "The Profits from Publishing: A Publisher's Perspective," *The Bookseller* (March 2, 2018), www.thebookseller.com/blogs/profits-publishing-publishers-perspective-743231#.

Literary Guild guarantee[d] a minimum sale of ... 500,000 to 600,000 copies."[63] Furthermore, as we will see in more detail later, many of the big book clubs were part of media and publishing conglomerates, which means that the benefits of scale were possible within the book club structure but also, on a higher level, within the whole conglomerate. It seems that the Literary Guild, for instance, preferred to select books published by Doubleday, its owner.[64] Similar patterns were visible within the multimedia conglomerate Holtzbrinck: the Deutscher Bücherbund book club often featured the best-selling books from the Holtzbrinck-owned publishers Fischer and Rowohlt.[65] Indeed, some of the book clubs were "vertically operated by one firm from papermaking to sales."[66]

Thompson's fifth point relates to taking economic risks. The clubs could calculate differently because they had guaranteed income through membership fees and contractual purchases. Thus, clubs could implement risky strategies such as "loss leading."[67] Lynette Owen describes loss leading as the "normal model of recruitment" for book clubs: "The initial offer is a book or a selection of books at a nominal price; such offers are called premiums and are loss leaders for the book clubs." These premiums spoke directly to prospective book owners: "a boxed set of a famous children's series, three lavish art books or a set of desk reference books traditionally generated a significant number of new members."[68] To quote another cartoon: Charles Schulz references such premiums in a 1971 Peanuts strip: Snoopy is proud of a multivolume set of fiction books – "the bonus for joining the Beagle Book Club."[69]

Typically, book clubs would advertise these boxed sets with an emphasis on the design and binding. For instance, the BOMC touted its "beautiful

---

[63] Kappel, "Book Clubs," p. 244. [64] Ibid., p. 245.

[65] Cf. see also, "Gute Nase," *Spiegel*, 27 (Oct. 22, 1973), 43, 99–104.

[66] D. E. Strout, "Book Club Publishing," *Library Trends*, 7 (1958), 1, 66–81, 66.

[67] See also "Loss Leader" in Law (ed.), *A Dictionary of Business and Management*, www.oxfordreference.com/view/10.1093/acref/9780199684984.001.0001/acref-9780199684984-e-3844.

[68] L. Owen, *Selling Rights*, 5th edn. (Abingdon: Routledge, 2006), p. 162.

[69] C. Schulz, "Beagle Book Club," in *Peanuts* (April 8, 1971), archived in *GoComics*, www.gocomics.com/peanuts/1971/04/08.

library volumes"[70] and "valuable library sets for $1 a volume" in *LIFE* magazine.[71] The Classics Club advertised its "Beautifully Bound, Lavishly Illustrated" editions and noted in the fine print that these were "uniform Classics Club bindings," "lovely volume[s] to [add to] your home library now."[72] In the 1970s, the BOMC still maintained that its premium of four books for $1 for new members was a sensible investment in future members.[73] However, in later years, clubs disclosed that high expenses for membership recruitment, including loss leading, were no longer sustainable – by 1970, for instance, Bertelsmann stated that it was averaging an unsustainable 100 DM investment for the recruitment of a new member through giveaways and loss leading and could really only afford to spend 55 DM.[74]

2.3 Cultural Impact of Book Clubs

The cultural influence that book clubs have had may be hard to measure precisely, but there are clear markers of the bearing of book clubs on book culture and society that transcend national markets. As David Carter describes, subscription book clubs and similar "middlebrow" endeavors had a distinct "dual commitment to culture and to its wider diffusion."[75] In 1927, an advertisement for the BOMC stated, "everyone who subscribes . . . (out of pure self-interest, because of the convenience and enjoyment . . .) may have the satisfaction of knowing that, by joining this movement, indirectly he is playing a role in stimulating our literature and deepening

[70] BOMC, "Beautiful Library Sets" [advertisement], *LIFE*, 21 (Nov. 25, 1946), 22, 3.

[71] BOMC, "Your choice of valuable library sets" [advertisement], *LIFE*, 49 (Nov. 14, 1960), 20, 8–9.

[72] The Classics Club, "Free as a trial-membership gift from The Classics Club" [advertisement], *LIFE*, 15 (Nov. 8, 1943), 19, 5.

[73] Cf. T. Weyr, "The Booming Book Clubs," in *The Business of Publishing* (New York: Bowker, 1976), pp. 259–85, 264.

[74] See also "Kaufen können: Verlage / Fusionen," *Spiegel*, 24 (April 27, 1970) 18, 241.

[75] D. Carter, "Middlebrow Book Culture," in M. Savage and L. Hanquinet (eds.), *Routledge International Handbook of the Sociology of Art and Culture* (New York: Routledge, 2015), pp. 349–69, 355.

our culture."[76] While this is, of course, adspeak, it emphasizes the widespread scholarly agreement and "unanimity of opinion throughout the industry"[77] that book clubs had a cultural impact by increasing the number of readers in society. This observation was confirmed and reiterated for American, British, Dutch, German, and other markets. For instance, Hutter and Langenbucher conducted a study of six German book clubs in the 1970s, stating that it is "indisputable that book clubs have brought the medium book into social strata which it either didn't or only hardly reached beforehand."[78] Hutchens was similarly clear on this point: "Thanks to the book clubs, ... more Americans are reading more books than have ever read books before. No one seriously disputes this, or really doubts that the clubs have performed a service in encouraging the reading habit."[79]

In 1981, Bernhard Meier showed that children living in households with a parent who was a book club member were more likely to be members in book clubs themselves and, regardless of a membership in a children's book club, were more likely to read regularly than children whose parents were not members; furthermore, the children were also more likely to read more diversely and more often.[80] This is unsurprising given the ample research available today, which emphasizes the significance of book ownership in households for later bookishness and academic success of children growing up in those households.[81]

---

[76] BOMC, "The Book-of-the-Month Club, *An outline of a unique plan for those who wish to keep abreast of the best books of the day* [brochure] (New York: BOMC, 1927), p. 4.

[77] Kappel, "Book Clubs," p. 245.

[78] "Es ist heute unbestritten, daß die Buchgemeinschaften das Medium Buch in Bevölkerungsschichten brachten, die es vorher nicht oder kaum erreichte." Hutter and Langenbucher, *Buchgemeinschaften und Lesekultur*, p. 9.

[79] Hutchens, "For Better or Worse, the Book Clubs," p. 1.

[80] Cf. pp. W1432/W1518–9 (tables 2.347/2.365) in B. Meier, "Leseverhalten unter soziokulturellem Aspekt," *Archiv für Soziologie und Wirtschaftsfragen des Buchhandels* (March 27, 1981), LI, W1327–407; (Aug. 21, 1981), LII, W1411–98; (Sept. 1, 1981), LIII, W1503–86.

[81] Cf. M. D. R. Evans, J. Kelley, and J. Sikora, "Scholarly Culture and Academic Performance in 42 Nations," *Social Forces*, 92 (2014), 4, 1573–1605, and, more

Furthermore, from the point of view of creating additional cultural value, membership in a book club could offer a means of identification and community building. In the twentieth century and into the twenty-first, there were book clubs for different genres such as crime and mystery,[82] but also for every thinkable and unthinkable niche group of society, from politics to religion to special interest. Joining a particular book club could be construed as (re-) affirmation of belonging to a community or a specific demographic group. Historically, as we will see in more detail later (Section 3.1), some of the first book clubs had their origins in political or social movements. The Büchergilde Gutenberg, for instance, was founded in 1924 as a nonprofit organization by the educational committee of the German printers' union.[83] The idea was to offer workers in the printing industry (and beyond) affordable books of high quality (concerning both content and design). Membership could also be an expression of fandom or preference for a certain genre. For instance, in 1984, the UK saw the inception of the über-specialized Cricket Book Club (Book Club Associates [BCA]) "for cricket lovers."[84] Other examples are military-themed clubs like the Military Book Club (US, Bookspan, founded in 1969, still in existence) and the Military Book Society (UK, BCA, later known as the Military and Aviation Book Society). Book clubs also catered to specific demographics like the book club Black Expressions (Bookspan, founded in 1999, discontinued in 2014, circa 500,000 members at its peak[85]) or to specific groups like the religious book club Crossings: Books You Can Believe In (Bookspan, founded in 1992, still

recently, J. Sikora, M. D. R. Evans, and J. Kelley, "Scholarly Culture: How Books in Adolescence Enhance Adult Literacy, Numeracy and Technology Skills in 31 Societies," *Social Science Research*, 77 (2019), 1–15.

[82] For a brief overview of the history of book clubs in relation to this genre, cf. J. L. Solberg, "Book Clubs," in R. Herbert (ed.), *The Oxford Companion to Crime and Mystery Writing* (Oxford: Oxford University Press, 1999), pp. 43–4.

[83] Bildungsverband der Deutschen Buchdrucker.

[84] Cricket Book Club, "The NEW book club . . . " [advertisement], *Times* (June 26, 1984), 25.

[85] Cf. H. Covington, *Literary Divas: The Top 100+ Most Admired African-American Women in Literature* (Phoenix, AZ: Amber, 2006), p. 86.

in existence). In 1988, BCA (then jointly owned by Doubleday/ W. H. Smith) had a portfolio of twenty-two book clubs;[86] Bookspan in 2001 (then still jointly owned by Bertelsmann and Time Warner) offered more than forty memberships.[87] By comparison, in 2019, Bookspan operated eight distinct clubs, plus the Book-of-the-Month subscription box service (see Section 4).

In his article, Hutchens glosses over a large-scale cultural discussion when he admits that some critics did not consider the book clubs to be "good for the national culture," claiming that they only "strain[ed] the presses and enriche[d] authors, publishers and book club operators."[88] With his observations, Hutchens swept an episode that later became known as the "Book Club War" under the carpet. Critics, especially in the late 1920s, and again in the 1950s, scathingly reported about the alleged industrialization of book distribution and the mass production of "books on the belt."[89] Book club operators were attacked for selling "conveyor-belt culture."[90] The criticism implicit in the use of this term clearly points to Theodor W. Adorno's work about the "culture industry."[91] Adorno's work is fundamental to understanding the contemporary reception of book clubs not only within the industry but also within society. Building on Adorno and writing about what he termed the "industrialization of the mind," the German philosopher and cultural critic Hans Magnus Enzensberger published a contribution about the paperback book series boom in West Germany in the 1950s. In this contemptuous critique of contemporary publishing practices, he did not refrain from commenting on the role of

---

[86] Cf. Monopolies and Mergers Commission (from now on abbreviated as M&MC), *Book Club Associates and Leisure Circle. A Report on the Merger Situation* (London: HM Stationery Office, 1988), p. 49.

[87] Arnold, "Making Books."

[88] Hutchens, "For Better or Worse, the Book Clubs," p. 1.

[89] Whipple, "Books on the Belt."

[90] Harker, *America the Middlebrow*, p. 16, referencing Radway, *A Feeling for Books*, p. 211 (though mis-referenced by Harker as p. 208).

[91] Cf., e.g., T. W. Adorno, "Résumé über Kulturindustrie," in R. Tiedemann and T. W. Adorno (eds.), *Gesammelte Schriften* (Frankfurt/Main: Suhrkamp, 2003), pp. 337–45.

book clubs within a "development of the publishing sector towards methods employed by big industrialist consumer goods manufacturing."[92] Enzensberger decried the fact that "digest extracts, book club editions and paperback editions are planned before the first line [of the book] has been typed."[93] Unsurprisingly, perhaps, Adorno's work also heavily informed Dwight MacDonald's essay *A Theory of Mass Culture*. As Joan Shelley Rubin argues, MacDonald's "dismissive" critiques obscured the cultural significance of the middlebrow from academic view, and "licensed the scholarly neglect" thereof.[94] From a perspective of book club history, MacDonald's most important and polarizing contributions are his comments about the BOMC judges and club choices being decidedly "midcult," which Radway treats in her book.[95] MacDonald is also known well for his derisive *New Yorker* pieces, including a blistering review of what he called the Book-of-the-Millenium Club: the Great Books of the Western World, which was actually a subscription for a fifty-four-volume set of texts.[96]

Interestingly, in a 2011 *New Yorker* contribution, Louis Menand argued that "Macdonald's mighty takedowns of middlebrow enterprises" may have in fact "inoculated *The New Yorker* against accusations of being middlebrow" itself.[97] This only confirms the impression that the categories high-, middle- and lowbrow are relative, if not arbitrary to a certain degree. These critical approaches from the Frankfurt School and its followers and

---

[92] "Diese Entwicklung des Verlagsgeschäfts auf die Methoden der großindustriellen Konsumgüterfertigung hin." H. M. Enzensberger, "Bildung als Konsumgut: Analyse der Taschenbuch-Produktion," in H. M. Enzensberger (ed.), *Bewußtseins-Industrie* (Frankfurt/Main: Suhrkamp, 1964), pp. 134–66, 142.

[93] "Digest-Extrakte, Nachdrucke für Buchgemeinschaften und Taschenbuchlizenzen für die ganze Verlagsproduktion werden verplant, noch bevor die erste Zeile steht." Ibid., pp. 141–2.

[94] J. S. Rubin, *The Making of Middlebrow Culture* (Chapel Hill, NC/London: University of North Carolina Press, 1992), p. xv.

[95] Radway, *A Feeling for Books*, pp. 189 and 310.

[96] Cf. D. MacDonald, "The Book-of-the-Millennium Club," *New Yorker*, XXVIII (Nov. 29, 1952), 41, 171–88.

[97] L. Menand, "Browbeaten. Dwight Macdonald's War on Midcult," *New Yorker*, LXXXVII (Sept. 5, 2011), 26, 72–8, 77.

successors have been picked up and repurposed by media studies scholars[98] but have been relegated to the historical archive by most book historians.

In her landmark study of the BOMC, Janice Radway also situates these cultural debates within questions of gender and the transformation of literary production in the first half of the twentieth century.[99] In her equally groundbreaking study, Joan Shelley Rubin traces the roots of middlebrow culture back to the nineteenth century, identifying the "Victorian preoccupation with the cultivation of character"[100] and Arnoldian ideas of culture as forerunners to book clubs' emphasis on personality development and character improvement.[101]

Aside from the cultural-theoretical discussions, in several national markets, cultural policy and book trade agreements reflected the impact of book clubs on widening readership by exempting the clubs from existing fixed book price agreements. Book club history is firmly intertwined with the history of fixed book price agreements such as the UK Net Book Agreement (1900 to 1997) or the German Buchpreisbindung (industry agreement since 1888, law since 2002): as long as booksellers cannot offer discounts to their clients, book club membership is an exclusive opportunity to have access to discounted books.[102]

A central question that is raised repeatedly across all national markets is whether book clubs are competitors or whether "sales through the mail generally complement and stimulate business" for traditional booksellers.[103] Book industry members and economists once postulated the "two markets theory."[104] Proponents of the theory were convinced that booksellers and

---

[98] Cf., e.g., S. Lash and C. Lury, *Global Culture Industry* (Cambridge: Polity, 2007).

[99] Radway, *A Feeling for Books*, pp. 210–20.

[100] J. S. Rubin, "Middlebrows," in I. Takayoshi (ed.), *American Literature in Transition, 1920–1930* (Cambridge: Cambridge University Press, 2018), pp. 43–60, 43.

[101] Rubin, *The Making of Middlebrow Culture*, esp. pp. 1–33.

[102] Regarding the Net Book Agreement, cf. Stevenson, *Book Makers*, pp. 1–29. For Germany, cf. P. Lutz/V. Titel, "Preisbindung," in U. Rautenberg (ed.), *Reclams Sachlexikon des Buches*, 3rd edn. (Stuttgart: Reclam, 2015), pp. 315–6.

[103] Appelbaum, "Paperback Talk. Sales Through the Mails," p. 31.

[104] "Zwei-Märkte-Theorie" (German). Not to be confused with the financial term "two-sided market." Regarding the proliferation of the theory in the

book clubs catered to two distinct markets, with consumers who bought books from bricks-and-mortar bookstores and consumers who were book club members as fundamentally different types of consumers and readers without overlap.[105] Book clubs even argued that they were a "breeding pond"[106] for nonreaders to grow into readers.

From the 1920s into the 1950s and 1960s, the two markets theory might apply. For the later stages, we have research that repudiates it. During the later decades of the twentieth century, book clubs were simultaneously competing with other actors in the industry (publishers, wholesalers, booksellers) but were also reliant on publishers for licenses to publish and/or distribute. For publishers and authors, this was not just a question of cultural enrichment but also an economic question. Did book clubs in fact generate additional income from licensing, or did the income from licensing undercut income from trade sales? Did the additional media attention and promotion perhaps stimulate sales of trade editions?[107] In the heyday of book clubs, licensing deals with book clubs meant very important additional revenue. Even around 2000, in a survey regarding the profitability of various distribution channels, "US [publishing] executives cited book clubs and wholesalers as their most profitable outlet, that is, the channel offering the greatest margin per unit sales."[108] In general, a book club deal was an asset. Hutter and Langenbucher state that in most cases, publishers welcomed book club editions as additional income, avoiding book club editions only for big brand names and products such as the *Duden* (the most important German spelling dictionary).[109]

  Netherlands, cf. H. Siebenga, *Boekenclub en boekhandel; wedijverende verkoopkanalen* (Tilburg: Katholieke Universiteit Brabant, 1987), esp. p. 2.

[105] Cf. Kollmannsberger, *Buchgemeinschaften im deutschen Buchmarkt*, p. 80.

[106] "Kweekvijver-Theorie," cf. Siebenga, *Boekenclub en boekhandel*, p. 2.

[107] Cf. J. L. W. West III, "The Expansion of the National Book Trade System," in C. F. Kaestle and J. A. Radway (eds.), *Print in Motion: The Expansion of Publishing and Reading in the United States, 1880–1940* (Chapel Hill: University of North Carolina Press, 2009), pp. 78–89, 83.

[108] Oda and Sanislo, *Book Publishing USA*, p. 79.

[109] Cf. Hutter and Langenbucher, *Buchgemeinschaften und Lesekultur*, p. 10.

In 1989, the *New York Times* published revealing numbers about the additional income generated by book club editions, specifically by book club deals with the BOMC. Traditionally, the article stated, authors received half of the licensing fee, which ran "from the low four figures for an alternate [selection] to the mid-five figures for a distinguished but not wildly commercial main selection."[110] The other half remained with the publisher. In addition to the licensing fee, the authors could hope for royalties (10 percent) if the advance earned out. Apparently, Stephen King withheld a novel from the clubs in the 1980s. According to the press, King was "convinced" that book club sales were reducing his retail sales. Tellingly, the following four King books were bought by the BOMC for approximately $1 million each. Industry insiders disclosed that the deal courted King with a share as high as 80 percent instead of the usual 50.[111]

From the outset of book clubs, there was no fixed book price agreement in the United States – ambitions for a fixed book price agreement had failed in 1913 with a Supreme Court verdict[112] – so there was no reason for the clubs to delay publication of their editions. The BOMC had introduced a simultaneous model and most other US clubs followed suit. In the UK with its Net Book Agreement, as in other markets with fixed price agreements, a delay of the book club edition was the norm. This delay could range from several months to a year. For instance, the Reprint Society's club World Books published its books a year after the original trade edition in the UK.[113] The successor of World Books, BCA, established simultaneous publication in the UK in the late 1960s.[114] In Germany, the typical delay was about six months, though this was subject to contractual negotiation, which included stipulations about the maximum difference in price

---

[110] J. Kaplan, "Inside the Club," *New York Times Magazine* (June 11, 1989), 62–8, 126–9, 62.

[111] Ibid., 62.

[112] Cf., e.g., M. Winship, "The Rise of a National Book Trade System in the United States," in Kaestle and Radway (eds.), *Print in Motion*, pp. 56–77, 64.

[113] Fitzgerald, *A Nickel an Inch*, p. 173.

[114] Cf. M&MC: *Book Club Associates and Leisure Circle*, p. 8.

between the original trade edition and the book club edition: the longer the delay in publication, the higher the price difference could be.[115]

2.4 Book Club Editions as Cultural Signifiers

Ursula Rautenberg's robust and far-reaching definition of the book circumscribes it in five respects, one of which is the book as a cultural object, as a signifier for attribution, social action, and rituals.[116] Sales numbers do not disclose how many people actually read the book club selections, using the book in its primary function as a text. The numbers do show that millions of book club editions filled bookshelves around the globe. Book clubs made starting, building, and expanding one's own book collection affordable.

Traditionally, book clubs propagated book ownership and thus often featured "elaborately cloth-bound volumes, making the advantageous price compared to the books available in the traditional bookstores obvious."[117] The book clubs were able to sell serious literature as well as commercial fiction. However, the key to selling these books was their design and the marketing – the literary content was one element, but not the only selling point. Especially in the early decades, the book clubs worked with hardcover and visually appealing, albeit only semi-valuable materials and design (cloth or sometimes leather, gilded edges, embossing, etc.) at a time when paperback books were on the rise: Albatross Books first appeared in Germany in 1931, Penguin Books was launched in the UK in 1935, and Pocket Books were first published in the United States in 1939.[118] Book club editions were marketed as

---

[115] Börsenverein des deutschen Buchhandels, *Preisbindungsrechtliche Kriterien für Buchgemeischaftsausgaben*, www.boersenverein.de/beratung-service/abc-des-zwischenbuchhandels/details/potsdamer-protokoll/.

[116] U. Rautenberg, "Buch," in *Reclams Sachlexikon des Buches*, pp. 65–8, 67.

[117] "aufwendige und in Leinen gebundene Ausgaben, wodurch ein offensichtlicher Preisvorteil gegenüber der Produktion des traditionellen Handels gegeben war." U. van Melis, "Buchgemeinschaften," in E. Fischer and S. Füssel (eds.), *Geschichte des deutschen Buchhandels im 19. und 20. Jahrhundert. Band 2: Weimarer Republik. Teil 2* (Berlin: De Gruyter, 2012), pp. 553–88, 554.

[118] A. McCleery, "The Book in the Long Twentieth Century," in L. Howsam (ed.), *The Cambridge Companion to the History of the Book* (Cambridge: Cambridge University Press, 2015), pp. 162–80, 165–7.

"expensive sets" or "furniture books." The "raw, unrefined quality of ... upstart literature" was outweighed by fancy bindings and the smell of leather-bound books. Members "bought the fine book sets ... not simply because they wanted to read them but also because they wished to display them as prized possessions."[119] This is a pattern visible throughout book club history. For instance, a Bertelsmann Lesering salesperson was quoted as saying about his potential customers that all Germans wanted was "a bunch of leather in their shelves."[120] Prospective members were enticed to join through loss leading, as mentioned earlier, but they were enticed to remain members through attractive volumes for relatively low prices. There was a close connection between book club membership and book ownership as well as book presentation.[121] This close relationship was emphasized by the book clubs through design. For instance, World Books wrote about its editions in its first advertisement in the *Times*, "Gratifying to handle, they are in craftsmanship equal to volumes at three times their price, and in appearance like expensive 'limited editions.'" The advertisement continued, "On your bookshelves they will make a decorative array, for though standard in size, the buckram cloth and leather labels will be in a harmonious variety of color."[122] In addition to matching bindings, book clubs also marketed book furniture. In the 1950s, for instance, one of the largest Dutch book clubs, the *Nederlandse Boekenclub* (NBC), rewarded fifteen recruitments of new members with a bookcase. The oak bookcase in the "Old English Mayflower" style was "designed precisely ... to fit 24 beautiful N.B.C. selections."[123]

[119] Radway, *A Feeling for Books*, pp. 159–60.

[120] See also "Die Bestsellerfabrik. Bertelsmann-Konzern," *Spiegel*, 11 (July 24, 1957), 30, 32–41, 32.

[121] On book clubs and book ownership, cf. also C. Norrick-Rühl, "Two Peas in a Pod: Book Sales Clubs and Book Ownership in the Twentieth Century," in E. Stead (ed.), *Reading Books and Prints as Cultural Objects* (Cham, Switzerland: Springer, 2018), pp. 231–50.

[122] World Books, "T. E. Lawrence's masterpiece ... " [advertisement], *Times* (Dec. 12, 1939), 4.

[123] According to the ad, the case was "pasklaar gemaakt voor zes N.B.C.-selecties. Het kan dus 24 kloeke boeken bevatten." See also "Een oud-engels boekenkastje cadeau," *Nieuws* (Jan.–Feb. 1953), 68, 6–7.

Another way to improve one's book presentation was to win a special book-case after suggesting good slogans for the NBC.[124] Similarly, in the 1950s, the Bertelsmann Lesering sold book furniture through the catalog *Heim und Buch*.[125]

In 1956, Bertelsmann Lesering members were asked about reasons for membership in a questionnaire that is preserved in the Bertelsmann archive. Besides the large selection (43 percent), the materials and design (30 percent) were mentioned most often, well ahead of the discounted price (18 percent).[126] Even after the postwar economic boom in Germany, the *Wirtschaftswunder*, subsided in the 1960s, Bertelsmann's Lesering still targeted "buyers primarily interested in book ownership," as demonstrated in a 1968 study.[127] This larger reading study also established that while book club members drew particular satisfaction from their book ownership and book collections, they did not necessarily draw satisfaction from the act of reading.[128] In 1969, another study indicated that one of the main objectives for book club membership was "interior decorating"[129] – a somewhat surprising wording that was confirmed in a 1980 examination, which showed that book club members value the book as an element of interior decorating and as a prestigious and precious possession, much more highly than customers in bricks-and-mortar bookstores.[130]

The book club editions, we can argue here, fulfill a large number of the qualities that collectible objects possess. In her book *On Collecting*, Susan

---

[124] See also "Boekenkasten voor Slagzinnen!," *Nieuws* (Jan. 1957), 107, 3–5; see also "Boekenkasten voor Slagzinnen," *Nieuws* (Feb. 1957), 108, 7.

[125] Cf. Lokatis, "A Concept Circles the Globe," p. 147.

[126] Cf. Bertelsmann Unternehmensarchiv 0041/6, 27, quoted in J. P. Holtmann, *Pfadabhängigkeit strategischer Entscheidungen. Eine Fallstudie am Beispiel des Bertelsmann Buchclubs Deutschland* (Cologne: Kölner Wissenschaftsverlag, 2008), p. 189.

[127] "vorwiegend am Buchbesitz interessierte[] Käufer[]." Bertelsmann Unternehmens-archiv-0006/73, 14–15, quoted in Holtmann, *Pfadabhängigkeit strategischer Entscheidungen*, p. 189.

[128] Kollmannsberger, *Buchgemeinschaften im deutschen Buchmarkt*, p. 89.

[129] Weissbach, "Buchgemeinschaften als Vertriebsform," p. 76.

[130] Cf. Hutter and Langenbucher, *Buchgemeinschaften und Lesekultur*, p. 11.

Pearce builds on Helga Dittmar's work on ownership of material objects. Dittmar proposes a social constructionist perspective on possessions and their role in the shaping of identity and shows that the reasons for prizing certain possessions vary with gender and socio-economic status. Based on an empirical study, Dittmar puts forward a coding system of reasons for possession of material objects. We can surmise that for many book club members, books were desirable for a combination of reasons. In Dittmar's terminology, books fulfilled an instrumentality (Dittmar's code: B2: "enables specific activity associated with object"). We can assume that many members primarily wanted to own the books to read them. Nevertheless, for book club members, the books also possessed "Qualities 'Intrinsic' to the Object" (Dittmar's code: A), such as "durability, reliability, quality" (A1) and "economy" (A2), and especially in the case of handsome volumes and boxed sets and similar product categories, "aesthetics" (A5). Additionally, books provided "enjoyment" (C: Other Use-Related Features, code C2), "entertainment or relaxation" (C3), and "information and knowledge" (C6). Additionally, bookshelves filled with an impressive number of volumes may have provided an outlet for "self-expression for others to see" (F2) and either as a "symbol for personal future goals" (F4) or as a "symbol for personal skills/capabilities" (F5) – which is why curated content was so important, so that the allegedly "right" books were on display. Finally, book ownership may also have contributed to "symbolic interrelatedness … with particular group(s)" (H3), that is, membership of and belonging to a community of like-minded readers.[131] Clearly, book club editions were collected, and presented, by the book club members themselves.

However, the collector's value of book club editions for posterity is contested. Some book club editions from clubs that publish(ed) their own original titles in specifically designed editions are valued (and valuable)

---

[131] Cf. H. Dittmar, "Meanings of Material Possessions as Reflections of Identity: Gender and Social-Material Position in Society," *Journal of Social Behavior and Personality*, 6 (1991), 6, 165–86, 175. See also S. Pearce, *On Collecting. An Investigation into Collecting in the European Tradition* (London: Routledge, 1995), pp. 208–9.

collectibles; some resale book clubs even offered their members limited access to signed first editions, such as the British club Modern First Editions (established in 1985[132]). Most run-of-the-mill book club editions from mass-market book clubs, however, are usually less valuable and less collectible. Two common themes on collector's websites and in book collector chat rooms are the worth of book club editions (often abbreviated as BCEs) and the difficulty of identifying them. The Antiquarian Booksellers' Association of America (ABAA) writes that a book club edition is "usually an inexpensive reprint utilizing poor quality paper and binding and sold by subscription to members of a book club; in general, of little interest to book collectors and of low monetary value."[133]

Book club editions are not an important part of rare book commerce for a number of reasons, though they may contribute to used book commerce. Firstly, first editions of titles might have had relatively low print runs, whereas first book club editions could have much higher print runs – book club editions are simply less rare and thus less interesting for collectors. Secondly, as emphasized by the ABAA, some book clubs saved money on their editions, using lighter paper grades or less elaborate bindings. This also lowers the value of the books. Thirdly, and most importantly, book club editions were usually preceded by a first trade edition, and collectors are often interested in the first-ever edition of a book. However, there are exceptions to this rule. In very select cases, some book clubs published exclusives or premieres, which meant that the books were only available to book club members for a certain amount of time before the first trade edition was published. Furthermore, some highly specialized book clubs like the Science Fiction Book Club (established in 1953, still in existence as part of Bookspan) published hardback editions of books that had hitherto only been published as mass-market paperback editions.[134] These first hardback editions

[132] E. J. Craddock, "Signs of Success," *Times* (May 27, 1985), 7.

[133] See also "Book club edition" in *ABAA Glossary of Terms*, www.abaa.org/glossary/entry/book-club-edition.

[134] For more context, cf. T. Doyle, "Collecting the Science Fiction Book Club," *BookThink. Resources for Booksellers* (Nov. 3, 2003), www.bookthink.com/0005/05sfb.htm.

can be collectible and certainly are better reading editions than first paperback editions, which can be quite fragile. Additionally, as several collectors confirm, in cases where a first trade edition is hard to come by or very expensive, contemporary book club editions can be valued highly as the next best thing: a kind of "trickle-down phenomenon."[135] Examples of this phenomenon are *To Kill a Mockingbird*, *The Catcher in the Rye*, or *Gone With the Wind*. Finally, book club editions may be attractive to collectors if the original dust jackets are still in good condition. The ABAA adds some other reasons for collecting book club editions as well: "variant cover art, the readability of the trim size, an interest in having different editions of a favorite title, or simply a desire to own an author's complete works in all formats."[136]

For the US market, book club editions can often be differentiated from regular trade editions through a blind stamp, "a small indentation or debossing"[137] of a geometrical shape (like a circle, diamond, or square) on the binding. Others can be identified by the paratexts on the dust jacket or an inlay of a book club review, which is often the case with the BOMC books. Identification of book club editions is less difficult in the UK, Germany, and other markets where non-simultaneous editions were the norm. Especially in Germany, the legal requirements surrounding the fixed book price mean that book club editions are required to diverge from the original edition in four points – the "magical square": (1) book club editions were only available to members, (2) the design had to be visibly different, (3) the editions could not be simultaneous, and (4) the price had to be different.[138] In Germany and similar markets, there are thus a number of

---

[135] C. Stark, "How to Identify Book Club Editions," *BookThink. Resources for Booksellers* (Nov. 6, 2008), www.bookthink.com/0005/05bce.htm.

[136] See also "Book club edition" in *ABAA Glossary of Terms*.

[137] Stark, "How to Identify Book Club Editions."

[138] M. Niewiarra and E. Gehrau, "Buchgemeinschaften und Wettbewerb," in P. Vodosek (ed.), *Das Buch in Praxis und Wissenschaft. 40 Jahre Deutsches Bucharchiv München; eine Festschrift* (Wiesbaden: Harrassowitz, 1989), pp. 263–94, 272. See also Kollmannsberger, *Buchgemeinschaften im deutschen Buchmarkt*, p. 205. The so-called Potsdamer Protokoll defines the relationship between book club editions and original publisher editions in Germany and states that regular book buyers should be able to identify the books as two

clear paratextual signs that books are book club editions to differentiate them substantially from the original editions. The book club has its own logo, which replaces the publisher's logo on the cover and binding; the binding quality and design are different, and so on. The best example of this for the German market is the Büchergilde Gutenberg, which, as mentioned briefly in Section 2.3, prides itself on its bibliophile but affordable editions. The club, which enhances the book club editions through design and illustrations, has won the German contest for the most beautiful book (Die schönsten deutschen Bücher, awarded since 1965) for more than 150 of its book club editions over the past decades.[139] The British Folio Society (established in 1947, sales to nonmembers since 2011,[140] membership system discontinued in 2016,[141] still in existence as a publisher of bibliophile editions today) had a similar brief, though the average products were more upscale and the focus on bibliophile and collector's editions was even more prominent than with the Büchergilde. Furthermore, the society mostly published classics, often preferring texts that were out of copyright to newer books that would have required payment of licensing fees.[142]

different editions. That is, typesetting and paper may be identical (enabling co-editions to be printed simultaneously), but not the binding and dust jacket. In cases of near-simultaneous or simultaneous publication of multiple editions, the difference must be even more marked than in regular cases with six months in between the original publication and the publication of the book club edition. Cf. Börsenverein, *Preisbindungsrechtliche Kriterien*.

[139] Cf. Büchergilde Gutenberg, "Prämierte Bücher" (2019), www.buechergilde.de /praemierte-buecher.html.

[140] Cf. E. Nawotka, "How the UK's Folio Society Is Changing with the Times," *Publishing Perspectives* (July 21, 2014), https://publishingperspectives.com /2014/07/how-the-uks-folio-society-is-changing-with-the-times/.

[141] Cf. S. Sutherland, "The Folio Society Is Ending Their Membership Program," *Alcuin Society Blog* (Aug. 19, 2016), http://alcuinsociety.com/folio-society-ending-their-membership-program/.

[142] For more context, cf. S. Rainey, "The Folio Society: Handsome Books at Minimal Cost," *The Courier*, 8 (1971), 3, 35–45.

Whether bibliophile editions from the Folio Society's zenith or paperback editions from the Quality Paperback Club,[143] from an inclusive standpoint not driven by antiquarian and rare book dealers, the most important principle of collecting applies to book club editions too: if there is a collector for the books, they are collectible – even if they are not valuable.

2.5 Suggesting a Theoretical Framework

As Leslie Howsam remarks, "[s]cholarship in book history has been peculiarly resistant to theory";[144] the German book historian Ursula Rautenberg would tend to agree.[145] But what does this mean for the analysis of book clubs within book history? Which theoretical underpinnings and models can we build on to reach a wider understanding of the workings and impact of book clubs within the twentieth-century book industry, within twentieth-century book culture, and as an element of twentieth-century social history more generally? Howsam adds elsewhere that "[n]o model has yet been introduced that can explain everything we need to know about the book in social, economic and cultural context."[146] This subsection aims to discuss and interweave different theoretical underpinnings suited to book club research.

This research considers book clubs to be part and parcel (pun intended) of what Ted Striphas calls "everyday book culture." Striphas defines book culture as the "meanings, values, practices, artifacts, and ways of life

---

[143] QPB, founded in 1974 and discontinued in 2015, was the "paperback baby" (Fitzgerald, *A Nickel an Inch*, p. 291) of the BOMC, later continued under BookSpan's direction. In 2015, all QPB members were transitioned to the Literary Guild. The last postings on the Facebook site (www.facebook.com /QPBBookClub/) are from 2015, though the site retains circa 7,000 fans/6,300 followers (status quo: November 2019).

[144] L. Howsam, *Old Books and New Histories. An Orientation to Studies in Book and Print Culture* (Toronto/Buffalo/London: University of Toronto Press, 2006), p. 39.

[145] Cf. U. Rautenberg, "Buchwissenschaft" in Rautenberg (ed.), *Reclams Sachlexikon des Buches*, pp. 100–103, esp. 102.

[146] L. Howsam, "Book History in the Classroom," in Howsam (ed.), *The Cambridge Companion to the History of the Book*, pp. 253–67, 263.

associated with books," and he emphasizes that when he is looking at "book culture," he is interested in "legal codes, technical devices, institutional arrangements, social relations, and historical processes whose purpose is to help secure ... book culture."[147] Building on Striphas's understanding of book culture, we can consider mail-order book culture to be the meanings, values, practices, and artifacts associated with choosing to receive and buy new books by mail rather than visiting a bookstore or a library.

Regarding the value of book clubs, as indicated in Section 2.3, different lines of inquiry have been prevalent over the past decades. Most importantly, however, book clubs are and have been framed as institutions of mass culture by literary and book historians, as discussed in detail by Joan Shelley Rubin in her book *The Making of Middlebrow Culture*.[148] Contemporary cultural critics used the term "middlebrow" to express their disdain of "upstart readers and reading practices" exemplified by book club members.[149] As Nicola Wilson, reading historian and expert for the British Book Society, writes, the term refers "both to a variety of genres and to its audience" and is "deliberately imprecise but generally understood as a kind of writing or experience that is inclusive and pleasurable but fundamentally inauthentic and conventional, middle-of-the-road."[150] In a double spread in 1949 based on a *Harper's* article by Russell Lynes, *Life* characterized "Everyday Tastes from High-Brow to Low-Brow." In the reading category, "book club selections" and "mass circulation magazines" corresponded to the "lower middle-brow."[151] The term, though not uncontested, is still widespread, and there is significant

---

[147] Striphas, *The Late Age of Print*, p. 10.

[148] Cf. Rubin, *The Making of Middlebrow Culture*, p. xv.

[149] T. Travis, "Print and the Creation of Middlebrow Culture," in S. E. Casper, J. D. Chaison, and J. D. Groves (eds.), *Perspectives on American Book History. Artifacts and Commentary* (Amherst: University of Massachusetts Press, 2002), pp. 339–66, 340.

[150] Wilson, "Middlemen, Middlebrow, Broadbrow," p. 317.

[151] See also "Everyday Tastes from High-Brow to Low-Brow Are Classified on Chart," *LIFE*, 26 (April 11, 1949), 100–101. Quoted in Travis, "Print and the Creation of Middlebrow Culture," pp. 348–9.

scholarly interest in the media formerly denounced as "middle-brow" today. In the *Routledge International Handbook of the Sociology of Art and Culture*, book historian David Carter notes the importance of acknowledgment of the "contentious history" of the terms; he also shows how newer work has found "some surprising parallels" between the concept of the "middlebrow" and sociologist Pierre Bourdieu's work.[152]

Book historians have recently relied more heavily on Bourdieu's work to better understand the industry and the relationships between the actors in what Bourdieu calls the "literary field" or the "field of cultural production."[153] Bourdieu's terminology and theories can help ask questions of the legitimization of book clubs and their role in selecting and thus (arguably) consecrating literature for their members (i.e., certain groups of readers). In her work on the Afrikaans book club the *De Burger-leeskring* (established in 1918, discontinued in 1925), Jana Klingenberg also draws on Bourdieu's theories. Klingenberg positions the Afrikaans book club in the South African field of cultural production, implementing Bourdieu's theory of capital to better understand the cultural impact (cultural capital) and commercial pressures (financial capital) that determined the role of the book club within the field.[154]

Recent discussions by German scholars have considered the potential of systems theory for book historical work, especially for the history of publishing. Axel Kuhn's suggestions for a historiography of publishing using a systems theoretical perspective are applicable to book publisher clubs as well.[155] In essence, his approach argues for an integrative view of

---

[152] Carter, "Middlebrow Book Culture," p. 349.

[153] P. Bourdieu, *Die Regeln der Kunst. Genese und Struktur des literarischen Feldes* (Frankfurt/Main: Suhrkamp, 1999), 227–57, 340–71.

[154] J. Klingenberg, "*De Burger-Leeskring*: a Brief History of South Africa's First Commercial Book Club and its Effect on Afrikaans Literature", *Quaerendo*, 49 (2019), 2, 158–179. I would like to thank J. Klingenberg for stimulating discussions on our panels at SHARP 2018 and at SHARP 2019.

[155] Cf. A. Kuhn, "Überlegungen zu einer systemtheoretischen Perspektive des Kulturbegriffs in der Verlagshistoriographie," in Norrick and Schneider (eds.), *Verlagsgeschichtsschreibung. Modelle und Archivfunde*, pp. 113–35, 115–24.

publishers within the social system of mass media, relating to other systems (politics, economics, art, and academia) depending on the types of books published. Considering the wide breadth of specialized book clubs for different demographic groups and/or for fans of any genre, this seems relevant to book club history as well. Kuhn's emphasis on internal decisions of publishers (economic versus aesthetic/artistic) and his call to widen the focus (from prosopography to other issues) are equally applicable to book club history.

A new model proposed by Sydney Shep, based on the approach of a *histoire croisée*,[156] is robust, but also flexible. It may be relevant to book club history in that it argues for an abstraction from national book historical inquiry and can underpin research on book clubs within what Shep calls the "event horizon." Book club research can profit from comparative studies into the "biography of a book" (which Shep situates between prosopography and bibliography) and the placeography of certain book club models – and these spaces and places, to echo Shep's terms, are interconnected closely for the entire twentieth century. We will see throughout Section 3 that the industry experts were well informed and feuilleton journalists actively reported and compared activities in other national markets. The similarities between book club structures and history across continents are striking, and to a certain extent, Shep's model permits us to grasp and contextualize these as situated knowledge.[157] I would argue that for a deeper understanding of a distribution channel, we need to add economic history to the "zone of investigation" produced by prosopography, placeography, and bibliography. We also need to consider prosopography in a wider way, looking beyond author prosopography and including agents, editors, judges, book club managers, and conglomerate CEOs and other decision makers within the framework. These points will be discussed further and implemented in Section 3.

---

[156] For more context, cf. M. Werner and B. Zimmermann, "Beyond Comparison: Histoire Croisée and the Challenge of Reflexivity," *History and Theory*, 45 (2006), 1, 30–50.

[157] S. Shep, "Books in Global Perspectives," in Howsam (ed.), *The Cambridge Companion to the History of the Book*, pp. 53–70, 65.

Another new model for book industry research was developed by Simone Murray, whose matrix diagram of the digital literary sphere gives us insight in yesterday's and today's book industry. Murray's matrix diagram captures "English-language literary culture at a key period of transition, when the influence of the old ways perceptibly remains but the logics of the new, digital environment have wrought such changes that the digital can no longer be regarded as a mere supplement to inherited print-culture structure."[158] As we will see, book clubs still active today engage in all five types of processes that Murray identifies for traditional literary institutions and organizations.

Different layers of theory and different models can be applied to book clubs to more fully understand the role they have played within the book industry and in society, contributing to an increase in readership and book ownership. The next section will offer a historical narrative of book clubs, highlighting "patterns and principles" within the long twentieth century in accordance with Alistair McCleery's recent challenge to book historians to move away from idiographic toward nomothetic analysis.[159] Throughout book club history, as in publishing history more generally, there are "earlier patterns [that] have been effaced by change, but nevertheless can be discerned through the intervening layers of business and cultural practice"; McCleery uses the metaphor of "palimpsest" to describe these traces.[160]

Throughout the following section, I will foreground four benefits of and reasons for book club membership that resurface regularly. I would like to introduce these four elements as the four Cs of book clubs: curation, convenience, concession, and community. Economists today differentiate three types of subscriptions: (1) access subscriptions such as Spotify or Netflix; (2) replenishment subscriptions, for instance, for dog food, coffee, or hygiene products; and (3) most importantly for us in our context here, curation subscriptions. In his book *Curation*, Michael Bhaskar writes, "In a world of too much, selecting, finding and cutting down is valuable. In the context of excess, curation isn't just a buzzword. It makes sense of the

---

[158] Murray, "Charting the Digital Literary Sphere," p. 320.

[159] McCleery, "The Book in the Long Twentieth Century," p. 163.

[160] Ibid., p. 162.

world."[161] Curation in this sense applies to any sort of selection of products for a specific demographic or for an individual. Historically speaking, every generation was overwhelmed by excess, compared to the generation before: "The roots of information overload run deep."[162] Hence, while the word "curation" may seem anachronistic when used to describe the club membership benefits for early-twentieth-century readers, it is accurate at second glance. Later in the historical overview, we will also see that some book clubs such as the Reader's Digest Condensed Editions Book Club additionally offered condensation of existing works – a more specific form of curation. The importance of the two Cs convenience and concession is almost self-explanatory: in capitalist systems, consumers covet the best-quality product at the lowest possible price and with the lowest possible effort. For decades and centuries, inventions and developments have been driven by the search for more convenient, cheaper solutions without (or with the lowest possible) compromise in quality. The fourth C, community, is a member benefit that clubs have implemented and communicated differently over the past 100 years: a sense of belonging to a movement. I will briefly discuss in Section 4 how the clubs that are still in existence today are putting more focus on the element of community than ever before.

3 Books for the Masses – Book Clubs in the Twentieth Century

The goal of this section is to offer a succinct history of book clubs for the long twentieth century, integrating and adapting Shep's approach to the material objects at hand – book club editions – and their producers and distributors – the book clubs themselves. We can draw on material from a variety of archival contexts (bibliography) and on (auto)biographical documentation by book club judges, editors, and managers (prosopography) and analyze individual examples (biography of a book). The aim is to

[161] M. Bhaskar, *Curation. The Power of Selection in a World of Excess* (London: Piatkus, 2016), p. 21.

[162] Ibid., p. 18.

work toward an understanding of book clubs within the "event horizon" situated between individual spaces and places (placeography: individual national book industries). To anchor the model more fully in the history of the book as a commodity, we can add an additional perspective of economic history to the event horizon, looking at mergers and acquisitions, for instance. The four Cs of book clubs will be interwoven into the narrative, showcasing the overarching similarities across national contexts.

3.1 Nineteenth-Century Precursors

The idea of subscribing to books is older than book clubs are, and the "book club is not a twentieth-century invention."[163] The earliest forms of subscription publishing are documented for the mid-sixteenth century.[164] For publishers or indeed for authors, soliciting subscriptions or advance payment (i.e., prenumeration) was a way to reduce the risks of publishing. During the height of subscription publishing from about 1770 to 1820, about one-sixth of all books were published with the support of prospective readers, who underwrote the book, thus promising to buy it – to support it in advance of publication. Pamela Selwyn argues that besides "securing the capital for paper and printing," prenumeration may also have been used to tap into new markets – much like the book clubs later did.[165] However, Günter Fetzer notes that distribution – especially beyond the existing networks of an author or publisher – was always a challenge.[166] In twenty-first-century terms, this could be viewed as a form of crowdfunding, though

---

[163] J. Barzun, "Foreword: Three Men and a Book," in A. Krystal (ed.), *A Company of Readers: Uncollected Writings of W. H. Auden, Jacques Barzun, and Lionel Trilling from the Readers' Subscription and Mid-Century Book Clubs* (New York: Free Press, 2001), pp. ix–xvii, ix.

[164] Cf. B. Findlay, "Subscription Publishing," in Suarez and Woodhuysen (eds.), *The Oxford Companion to the Book*, vol. 2, pp. 1186–7.

[165] Cf. P. Selwyn, *Everyday Life in the German Book Trade* (University Park: Pennsylvania State University Press, 2000), pp. 75–8 for an overview of advantages and disadvantages of the system.

[166] G. Fetzer, "Selbstverlag," in Rautenberg (ed.), *Reclams Sachlexikon des Buches*, pp. 364–5, 364.

these types of subscription are generally understood to be precursors of self-publishing.

Besides a reduction of risks for the author and publisher, subscription publishing significantly reduced the dependence on book distribution infrastructure (bookstores, booksellers). Michael Hackenberg has convincingly argued that the subscription publishing network in the nineteenth century enabled "millions of books" to be read in the "American heartland."[167] As delineated earlier (Section 2.2), reliable mail and delivery infrastructure was necessary to conduct any business by mail, including subscription publishing models. However, subscription publishing cannot be considered convenient for the readers: they had to subscribe to each book individually and be well informed or part of an existing network of well-informed and well-connected readers. The publishers soliciting subscribers did not offer curation.

Several contenders vie for the title of the first book club in a modern sense. A precursor to the German book clubs that in turn became the "archetype"[168] for modern book clubs worldwide is the Verein zur Verbreitung guter katholischer Bücher, which was founded in 1829 and emphasizes the element of curation in its name: the Society for the Distribution of Good Catholic Books. The Litterarische Verein in Stuttgart (the Literary Society in Stuttgart) followed ten years later in 1839. The Bibliothek der Unterhaltung und des Wissens (the Library of Entertainment and Knowledge) was established in 1876 and was the direct precursor of the large German book club Deutscher Bücherbund (later bought by Holtzbrinck and merged with the Stuttgarter Hausbücherei). However, the Verein der Bücherfreunde, founded in 1891 in connection with the working-class self-education movement (Arbeiterbildungsbewegung), is often considered the first modern book sales club in Germany. Most of the early, pre-World War I (WWI) book clubs had subscription models slightly differing from the later, post-WWI membership model, with the element of curation of titles that grew to success in Germany first, quickly followed by Europe and overseas. Still, with its political and idealistic outlook, the Verein

---

[167] M. Hackenberg, "The Subscription Publishing Network in Nineteenth-Century America," in Hackenberg (ed.), *Getting the Books Out*, pp. 45–75, 66.

[168] Strout, "Book Club Publishing," p. 66.

der Bücherfreunde pioneered a model of success and already emphasized the elements of community and curation.[169]

3.2 Book Club Beginnings in the Interwar Period

A combination of factors in post-WWI Germany congealed to form the perfect basis for the development of the modern book sales club.[170] The aftermath of WWI saw a diversification of society – culturally, politically, religiously, and ideologically. Stratification of society into educated and non-educated groups, and straightforward marketing toward the educated and the wealthy was no longer sufficient. Existing publishing firms and traditional bookselling structures, however, were encrusted in their traditional worldview and proved slow to change. For instance, books targeted toward working-class readers were simply unavailable in traditional bookstores, which explains the rapid establishment of seven book clubs catering to the needs of working-class readers in Germany alone. For specific groups of readers, book clubs were framed as alternatives operating independently of the traditional book distribution infrastructure.

After WWI in Germany, book prices were higher than they had been in the prewar period, and the prewar book price agreements stayed in place. The new book clubs circumvented the book price agreements with their membership structure and were able to offer books for significantly lower prices: the element of concessions was clearly important to the new readers. Urban van Melis exemplifies the advantageous rates. Regular book editions cost an average of 4.78 Reichsmarks (RM) in 1925, and prices increased steadily to 5.55 RM in 1927 and 6.26 RM in 1930. By charging 1 RM a month and offering their members four books for that price, the book club editions cost an average of 3 RM – and the membership price was lowered by many book clubs in the later 1920s.

As Urban van Melis shows, forty-two book clubs were founded between 1918 and 1933 in Germany. The two most important at the time were the Volksverband der Bücherfreunde in 1919, which amassed 750,000 members by 1931, and the Deutsche Buch-Gemeinschaft, which had more than 400,000

---

[169] This paragraph follows E. Henze, "Buchgemeinschaften," in S. Corsten, S. Füssel, and G. Pflug (eds.), *Lexikon des gesamten Buchwesens* (LGB²), 2nd edn. (Stuttgart: Hiersemann, 1987), vol. I: A–Buch, pp. 592–7.

[170] These three paragraphs follow van Melis, "Buchgemeinschaften," pp. 553–6.

members by 1930. The Volksverband der Bücherfreunde was a publisher book club, which offered its members new editions of texts by contemporary authors that had not been published previously as individual titles. Originally, members were obliged to buy the quarterly book without so much as a negative option, but the club proved member-friendly and adaptable and changed its conditions quickly. By the 1930s, members had an extremely convenient method of access to curated content at low prices: they were only obliged to spend 2.90 RM every quarter. The Volksverband der Bücherfreunde emphasized the accessibility of books but also included books in a large range of prices in its list, from an astounding 0.40 RM for nonfiction books bound in cloth to the half-leather bindings (2.90 RM) and nicer books up to approximately 5 RM. Interestingly, the Volksverband der Bücherfreunde also pointed its members toward a few more valuable book sets such as a two-volume encyclopedia for 36 RM or a Bible edition for 39 RM.

These developments did not go unseen in the US book industry. While WWI had not impacted US book distribution infrastructure the way it had in Europe,[171] access to books was still very limited for people living in non-urban areas. The numbers in the literature vary slightly, but the gist is similar: most Americans did not have direct access to books, and even those who had direct access did not have a good selection to choose from or were not the main clientele of the existing stores. Davis writes that there were 4,000 "places where a book could be purchased" (including gift shops and stationary stores with a small selection) and only approximately 500 dedicated bookstores, most of which were "refined, old-fashioned 'carriage trade' stores catering to an elite clientele in the nation's twelve largest cities."[172] Travis writes that there were fewer than 1,000 bookstores in the United States, most of these located in urban areas.[173]

---

[171] The early-twentieth-century history of book clubs in France is covered briefly by P. Riberette, "Les Clubs du Livre," *Bulletin des Bibliothèques de France* (1956) 6, 425–35, http://bbf.enssib.fr/consulter/bbf-1956-06-0425-003.

[172] K. C. Davis, *Two-Bit Culture: The Paperbacking of America* (Boston: Houghton Mifflin, 1984), p. 16.

[173] T. Travis, "Book Clubs (Distribution)," in Suarez and Woodhuysen (eds.), *The Oxford Companion to the Book*, vol. 1, pp. 546–7, 546.

The Literary Guild was originally incorporated in 1922, technically making it the first modern book club in the United States, but it did not begin its activities until 1927.[174] By then, former adman Harry Scherman had founded the BOMC (1926) with resounding success. BOMC is the focus of an overwhelming amount of scholarly attention for a number of reasons, only one of which is its status as the de facto first modern book club in the United States. Another reason is the availability of documents relating to its history. The large US media outlets reported on the status of the club in detail, and the club itself was quite professional in the areas of corporate history and history marketing, putting out commemorative brochures and books regularly. This ubiquity transferred into its status as a brand and household name. Ed Fitzgerald, president and CEO of the BOMC (1972 to 1984), wrote in his memoir, "The Book-of-the-Month Club is so much the dominant club in the business that all the book-club jokes are made about it."[175]

The key elements of BOMC founder Harry Scherman's idea were "Convenience; reading fulfillment; guidance by experts; continuity."[176] The system of guidance by experts has been discussed in detail by Lee and later by Radway and Rubin and will be sketched out here briefly. The system set the BOMC apart from similar endeavors, since the experts had no stake in the club and did not profit financially from the earnings of the club. Scherman's "Editorial Board" was composed of five public figures with an academic and/or literary background as well as social standing – at least some prospective members would have heard or read the judges' names before in different cultural contexts. These five judges were identified by the management of the club and worked together to choose "the best books as they appear" from preprint proofs submitted by US publishers.[177] The club also considered the editorial board as a "self-imposed buffer so that choices are not made merely for commercial reasons."[178] The first five judges were

---

[174] Cf. C. Lee, *The Hidden Public: The Story of the Book-of-the-Month Club* (New York: Doubleday, 1958), p. 15.

[175] Fitzgerald, *Nickel an Inch*, p. 267. [176] Lee, *The Hidden Public*, p. 29.

[177] BOMC, *An Outline of a Unique Plan . . .*, p. 5.

[178] H. Mitgang, "Head of Book-of-Month Club to Retire Next Month," *New York Times* (Dec. 28, 1978), C16.

the eminent scholar and critic Henry Seidel Canby as chairperson; the author, editor, and politician William Allen White; the novelist and critic Dorothy Canfield Fisher; the well-known newsperson Heywood Broun; and the literary star Christopher Morley. The judges represented different areas of the United States geographically (East Coast, Midwest, etc.) and different areas of interest and expertise thematically. With a view toward Shep's model, it becomes obvious that the life histories of these five judges in particular (as well as their resulting conceptions of and attitudes toward literature) have been the subject of an almost overwhelming amount of scholarly attention, fueling our understanding of book clubs and book commerce through the lens of prosopography.

According to club advertisements, the judges were guided by questions such as "Has this book real merit?" "Will it be considered readable and interesting and worth-while?"[179] With this preselection of titles, the BOMC promised to be the perfect organization for "individuals who are anxious to keep *au courant* with the best of new books as they are published, but who constantly neglect to do so through procrastination or because they are too busy."[180] As Travis summarizes, "the Book-of-the-Month Club acknowledged the twin dilemmas of the modern white-collar reader: the inability to keep up with the proliferation of information, and the simultaneous need to do so."[181] In fact, at inception, the club did not offer discounts to its members; the members originally paid the full price for their monthly book – membership was based solely on convenience and curation at first. Later, concessions were handed down from the management to the members.[182]

As delineated in Section 2, the negative option system was central to the economics of the club business to ensure benefits of scale and lower risks. The goal for the clubs had to be a high acceptance rate for the "Main Selection," because members could opt out of the "Main Selection" and buy an "Alternate" instead. In 1946, Scherman still assumed that the majority of members would not return Main Selections, expressing

---

[179] BOMC, *An Outline of a Unique Plan . . .*, p. 14.   [180] Ibid., p. 5.

[181] Travis, "Print and the Creation of Middlebrow Culture," p. 361.

[182] Radway, *A Feeling for Books*, p. 200.

surprise when only 43 percent of his members accepted a "Main Selection" in 1945.[183] Over the course of the decades, the average acceptance rate of the "Main Selection" changed significantly, as we will see in the subsequent sections.

Germany and the United Kingdom had fixed price agreements in common, but the first club to operate in the United Kingdom took its inspiration from the American system and the BOMC. In fact, a *New York Times* article stated, "it is apparent that these two English book clubs [i.e., the Book Society and its later British rival the Book Guild] are patterned as nearly as possible after the American clubs."[184] While Scherman was a man with a background in advertising, thus approaching the book as a commodity and marketing it as such, the Book Society had a different background. Two touchstones of culture for the 1920s, Sir Hugh Walpole and the novelist Arnold Bennett, established it in 1929, with Walpole acting as chairperson of a selecting committee, thus foregrounding curation as the most important element of the club, because "indiscriminate reading can be time-wasting and frustrating."[185] As Wilson writes, the Book Society quickly "achieved a membership and stature that made publishers, libraries, bookshops, and readers sit up and take notice."[186] Much like the BOMC, the Book Society did not grant members a discount at inception of the club, and the negative option model was copied as well. Book Society subscribers did not receive special book club editions. A regular "copy of the publisher's edition of the chosen book" was sent to subscribers, but it was adorned with a "Book Society choice" bellyband and the "books were announced as a 'Book Society choice' on the same day as the publication of the ordinary first edition." Besides the emphasis on curation, Wilson underlines the

---

[183] *Commodore Hornblower* by C. D. Forester. Cf. Hutchens, "For Better or Worse, the Book Clubs," p. 28.

[184] T. Macauley, "Book Club Debate Again On in England," *New York Times* (March 9, 1930), p. E3.

[185] Book Society, "this way … there's always time for a book" [advertisement], *Times* (Sept. 23, 1955), 10.

[186] N. Wilson, "Virginia Woolf, Hugh Walpole, the Hogarth Press, and the Book Society," *English Literary History*, 79 (2012), 1, 237–60, 244.

system's convenience for British subscribers: the "popular system," she writes, "made book-buying easy and convenient."[187] Another interesting argument Wilson makes is that the Book Society can be framed as Britain's "first celebrity book club," which is particularly interesting from a twenty-first-century perspective.[188]

Following the introduction of the modern paperback to the British book industry (with Penguin books in 1935), the first book club in Britain based on the German archetype as a discount book club was launched: the Readers Union (founded in 1937, dissolved in 2016) and recruiting thousands of members within weeks. There were discussions within and between both trade organizations, the Booksellers Association and Publishers Association, about the relationship between these types of book clubs and book commerce. The booksellers in particular worried about loss of clientele.[189]

The big clubs like the Volksverband der Bücherfreunde, the BOMC, Book Society, and Readers Union reached large proportions of the society, whereas smaller, niche clubs catered to segments of society and the reading interests of specific groups. An especially prominent development was the foundation of politically motivated book clubs, sometimes affiliated with political parties. As indicated earlier, book clubs for working-class readers were especially popular in 1920s Germany, tying into social democratic or socialist movements of the period. The Left Book Club in the UK (founded in 1936, discontinued in 1948, re-launched with a crowdfunding scheme in late 2015[190]) was "a scheme for the dissemination of politically educative

---

[187] Ibid.

[188] Wilson, The Book Society Site, About, https://thebooksocietysite.com /about/. On celebrity culture and book clubs today, see e.g. S. Marsden, "'I Didn't Know You Could Read.' Questioning the Legitimacy of Kim Kardashian-West's Status as a Cultural and Literary Intermediary," *Logos*, 29 (2018), 2–3, 64–79.

[189] Cf. Stevenson, *Book Makers*, p. 89.

[190] Cf. A. Flood, "Left Book Club Bids to Crowdfund Radical Reading, with Help of Chomsky," *The Guardian* (Oct. 20, 2016), www.theguardian.com/books/ 2016/oct/20/left-book-club-crowdfund-radical-reading-network.

literature," initiated by the publisher Victor Gollancz in collaboration with Harold Laski and John Strachey. The club was known for its pointed and provocative marketing[191] and "doctrinaire character" but also for the high intellectual standard of its books. At its peak, it had not only 56,000 members but also 1,500 affiliated "left discussion groups."[192] The success of the Left Book Club led to the foundation of The Right Book Club[193] in the UK, as well as the Labour Book Service and the Liberal Book Club – all indicative of the community element of the book club business. Membership was a way to express status, personal tastes, and political preferences – and to stock up on the ostensibly "appropriate" books as material expressions of belonging affordably.

This early diversification of the book club business by genre or interest group, demographics, and political affiliation is another similarity across different national markets. Besides the political clubs, religious clubs also played an important role. For instance, the Catholic Book Club was founded in the United States in 1928, curating the books "most representative of Catholic thought" for its members and thus reinforcing their sense of religious community as well.[194] Separate clubs for children were also founded quickly. The first children's book club was announced in November 1928 in the United States, to "aid parents in forming in their children a taste for good literature,"[195] and soon followed by others, among them a subdivision of the Literary Guild, the Junior Literary Guild (founded in 1929 and almost immediately merged with Selected Books for Juniors, Inc.). The setup mimicked the established clubs and

---

[191] Cf. J. Roscoe, "'The Age of Shouting Had Arrived,'" *Logos*, 29 (2018), 2–3, 9–25.

[192] See also "Left Book Club, The," in J. Stringer (ed.), *The Oxford Companion to Twentieth-Century Literature in English* (Oxford: Oxford University PressUniversity Press, 1996), p. 385.

[193] For more context, cf. T. Rodgers, "The Right Book Club: Text Wars, Modernity and Cultural Politics in the Late Thirties," *Literature & History*, 12 (2003), 2, 1–15.

[194] See also "Start Catholic Book Club," *New York Times* (April 23, 1928), 18.

[195] Established by the Association of Junior Leagues of America. See also "Literature for Youths. A Children's Book-of-the-Month Club to Be Organized," *New York Times* (Nov. 1, 1928), 23.

offered curation by experts and public figures such as Eleanor Roosevelt, who was a founding member of the Junior Literary Guild's advisory board.[196]

Across national book industries, one of the other likenesses is the antagonism that book clubs faced. In Shep's terminology, the event horizon contains clashes and confrontations between the traditional and conventional industry actors and stakeholders and the newcomers – the book clubs. On the one hand, as sketched out earlier, there were the early cultural critics, decrying the demise of art and culture through commodification and mass production, building up to Walter Benjamin and Theodor W. Adorno. On the other hand, there are parallels in the reactions of the traditional book industry players to the book clubs. The clubs "shook up the industry even as they increased the market for books,"[197] and the industry reactions ranged from panic and confusion to the foundation of book clubs in partnership with traditional publishers and booksellers, with the intent to weaken the new players.

In the German book industry, booksellers were clearly worried about the loss of customers.[198] Those that spoke out publicly reframed their worries in a patronizing way, explaining that only booksellers were able to select and recommend the proper books for individual readers, and the book industry could not fulfill its cultural role if there were too many players in the market. Allegedly, distribution of the same book to hundreds of thousands of readers underestimated and homogenized them. Instead of analyzing the success of the book clubs and learning from it, the book trade tried to fight the clubs. In 1925, Börsenverein des deutschen Buchhandels, the German booksellers' and publishers' association, was even involved in a boycott scheme, which resulted in heavy criticism from author organizations and the literary scene. From 1925 to 1927, a group of publishers and booksellers tried to launch its own book club with the Deutsche Buch-

---

[196] Cf., see also, "Two New Book Clubs for Children Merge," *New York Times* (Aug. 6, 1929), 26.

[197] A. Haugland, "Book Propaganda: Edward L. Bernays's 1930 Campaign Against Dollar Books," *Book History*, 3 (2000), 231–52, 233.

[198] Cf. van Melis, "Buchgemeinschaften," pp. 575–83.

Einkaufs-Gemeinschaft, which enabled members to buy books that no longer had a fixed price at a discount and made new publications available for a reduced price. Readers could join the Buch-Einkaufs-Gemeinschaft in participating bookstores and pick up their books there; the membership fee of 1.80 RM a month was split between the collecting bookstore (30 percent) and the club (70 percent). However, the booksellers were skeptical and by 1927, the Buch-Einkaufs-Gemeinschaft only had 5,000 members and had incurred high advertising costs, leading to insolvency.

UK publishers and the British trade organization Booksellers Association and Publishers Association had already had their share of industry drama with the "Book War" (1905–8), triggered by the *Times* book club scheme. This book club was in essence "a free lending library (thus challenging the circulating libraries) ... and in addition a discounting bookseller."[199] The book clubs were eyed with interest and worry, but some book industry members sprang onto the bandwagon. Following the foundation of the Book Society in 1929, the Readers Union was founded in 1937. This was followed in the same year by Foyle's The Book Club, a bookstore-club arrangement that guaranteed sales through the bookstores, predating Bertelsmann's signature shop-in-shop model by decades. William A. Foyle wrote in the *Times* in a self-advertisement masquerading as a letter to the editor: "There is no doubt that book clubs have come to stay in this country, as in other countries, and we feel that, as such is the case, they should be organized by a bookseller or publisher and not run by an outside organization."[200] John Feather shows that while the Associated Booksellers of Great Britain and Ireland was worried by possible competition from the clubs, the "publishers were always reluctant to interfere with book clubs in the 1930s, for they saw them as a valuable source of income."[201] In fact, endeavors such as Hutchinson's Universal Book Club[202] (founded in 1939, discontinued after 1951) or the Reprint

---

[199] Stevenson, *Book Makers*, p. 20.

[200] W. A. Foyle, "The New Writer" [letter to the editor], *Times* (Oct. 5, 1937), 10.

[201] J. Feather, *A History of British Publishing* (London: Routledge, 1988), p. 188.

[202] Universal Book Club, "Philipp Gibbs ... Join now – editions are limited" [advertisement], *Times* (Dec. 1, 1939), 4.

Society's World Books (founded in 1939, sold to W. H. Smith and Doubleday in 1966 and rebranded as Book Club Associates) were publisher-owned book clubs.[203] Overall, the discussions surrounding book clubs were less dramatic than in Germany in the 1920s and led to "a series of regulations governing the conduct of book clubs" in 1939.[204]

US publishers and booksellers were in a slightly different situation, since there was no fixed book price agreement to adhere to. Nonetheless, the US book industry experienced its own "book club wars." As Radway lays out, discussions were prompted by and embedded within more general questions of standardization versus choice. The mass culture debate raged in the newspapers and magazines.[205] Within the industry, "bookseller hostility was assured," and publishers closely observed the pros and cons of selection as a book club edition. In 1929, reacting to an incendiary statement of the American Booksellers' Association, Literary Guild president Harold Guinzberg cited ten years of success for the German book clubs and increasing numbers of German book titles, bookstores, and book sales, reinforcing the impression that the book industries learned from and mimicked one another.[206] By the 1940s, however, most booksellers acknowledged that book clubs "helped their sales."[207] In the United States though, clubs were free to grant additional membership bonuses in the form of free books, which was not possible in other national contexts with book price agreements. Under pressure during the Great Depression years to retain members, Scherman developed the idea of "Book Dividends" – free books for long-standing members if the business was thriving, similar to cash dividends offered by corporations. While the dividend system apparently buoyed the BOMC's membership throughout the Great Depression years, it caused additional aggravation in the industry,

---

[203] Cf. Feather, *A History of British Publishing*, p. 188.

[204] J. Baker, "Book Clubs," in J. Hampden (ed.), *The Book World today: A New Survey of the Making and Distribution of Books in Britain* (London: Allen & Unwin, 1957), pp. 120–7, 121.

[205] For more context cf. Radway, *A Feeling for Books*, pp. 198–260.

[206] Quoted in "Retailers Attack Book Club System," *New York Times* (May 14, 1929), 25.

[207] Strout, "Book Club Publishing," p. 68.

especially the advertisement of "free" books, which was later deliberated by the Federal Trade Commission.[208] The US clubs were eventually acquitted completely and were allowed to advertise using the word "free" after 1953.

Clandestine industry boycotts, codes of conduct, and cultural critique aside: by the advent of World War II (WWII), the book clubs were well established as an alternative form of distribution in the book industry. While these book clubs were mostly active within distinct national contexts, the individual clubs had members around the globe. The British book clubs in particular reached thousands of readers in the Commonwealth and other foreign countries – the Book Society, for instance, had members in more than thirty countries. Of course, the events of WWII heavily impacted the book industry – a topic that is far too complex to elucidate in detail here. For the book clubs, which were used to growth and expansion, the war was a phase of consolidation, and the main goal became maintaining the status quo. The war had practical consequences such as shortages and changes in personnel and reliance on paper rationing. Discounts and concessions became arguably more important during wartime, but consumers also focused on necessary products instead of leisure products.

The war also had ideological consequences influencing the curation element of the club. The war efforts were also visible in the selections: curated content for countries at war was different from curated content during peacetime. An analysis of translations chosen as BOMC Main Selections, for instance, shows that German titles by best-selling authors such as Erich Maria Remarque and Vicki Baum were very popular with the Editorial Board in the 1920s, while this changed into the 1930s and 1940s, when only books published by German authors in exile made the cut.[209]

The community element could be considered even more important in wartime, when people were facing insecurity and loss, especially in Britain and Germany. Some German clubs closed down or went into exile, such as the Büchergilde Gutenberg, though the Deutsche Buch-Gemeinschaft and

---

[208] For more context, cf. Lee, *The Hidden Public*, pp. 63–4 and Radway, *A Feeling For Books*, pp. 309–10.

[209] Cf. C. Norrick-Rühl, "Stimulating Our Literature and Deepening Our Culture," *Quaerendo*, 47 (2017), 3–4, 222–51.

the Volksverband der Bücherfreunde were in business until 1945, reaching approximately 1.7 million members in 1940.[210] In *Book Makers,* Iain Stevenson writes about WWII and the book trade, explaining that the war acted as a "catalyst, crystallizing and fixing the new directions made in the previous years" and also "creating new conditions" for the book trade to "successfully reinvent itself" in the immediate postwar period.[211] While Stevenson is referring to British book trade history, certain characteristics are transferable to other book industries as well.

3.3 The Book Club Boom from the Postwar Period into the 1960s

Book industry statistics were published more regularly across all markets beginning in the postwar period, and book historians can thus rely on a number of statistical analyses by contemporaries for this and for later phases. In 1956, the American Book Publishers Council distributed a survey to 108 US book clubs with a total of more than 7 million members. The survey showed clearly that the fluctuation during the postwar period was particularly high. Dozens of clubs were established, but often without longevity. Many clubs did not last more than three years, though BOMC and Literary Guild still dominated the market as long-standing competitors.[212]

For the same phase in the UK, John Baker names four major book clubs (Reprint Society, The Book Club, Readers Union, and Odhams' Companion Book Club) and approximately a dozen other book clubs. Baker states that UK "purchasing membership" in 1957 was at about 0.75 million books a month.[213] In 1955, the clubs had a "combined membership of over 900,000," reaching "a quarter of all British homes" and "extend[ing] the frontiers of reading."[214] The Net Book Agreement –

[210] Cf. Henze, "Buchgemeinschaften," p. 593.

[211] Stevenson, *Book Makers,* p. 107. [212] Strout, "Book Club Publishing," p. 72.

[213] Baker, "Book Clubs," p. 123.

[214] J. H. Barrett et al., "Postal Charges for Books" [letter to the editor], *Times* (Dec. 8, 1955), 11.

upheld in the Restrictive Practices Court in 1957 and 1962[215] – continued to enable book club growth in the UK.

For Germany, beginning in the 1950s, we have continuous data from *Buch und Buchhandel in Zahlen (BuBiZ)*. All of the statistics show that the postwar period is the fastest-paced phase in book club history. New clubs "mushroomed" across national book industries, and the existing clubs grew "at a pace that [made] of Jack's Beanstalk a late-blooming narcissus."[216] There is a scholarly consensus about the "especially favorable conditions of the era" for book club proliferation.[217] Many people who lost their homes and possessions during the war quite simply had a need to replace and rebuild, and a desire to surround themselves with symbols of stability and continuity: books and bookshelves.[218]

Speaking in Shep's terms, for this phase, the event horizon of book club history leans toward the economic history, though the life histories of prominent book club entrepreneurs like Reinhard Mohn influence the historical trajectory as well. In Germany, the 1950s were a phase of rapid recovery and rebuilding – the so-called *Wirtschaftswunder*. During this decade, through chance, clairvoyance, and aggressive mergers and acquisitions policies, companies and individuals in Germany laid the groundwork for today's highly concentrated global industry. The Bertelsmann Lesering, founded in 1950 (later renamed Bertelsmann Club), formed the roots for Bertelsmann's expansion as a global multimedia conglomerate. Bertelsmann's main national competitor, and one of the major players in the global media industry today, Holtzbrinck, also followed a similar trajectory from a book club business into a multimedia conglomerate with the Stuttgarter Hausbücherei (later merged with the Deutscher Bücherbund).

As sketched out in the previous section, a similarity across national market contexts was the level of unease and antagonism among booksellers, publishers, and book clubs. While the book clubs were undeniably established as players in the industry, unfavorable opinions and unspoken

---

[215] Stevenson, *Book Makers*, p. 285.

[216] Hutchens, "For Better or Worse, the Book Clubs," p. 1.   [217] Lokatis, p. 140.

[218] For more context, cf. L. Pyne, *Bookshelf* (New York: Bloomsbury Academic, 2016), passim, but esp. pp. 67–81.

stereotypes still hindered communication and cooperation. It is unclear whether Bertelsmann was familiar with Foyle's prewar book club scheme, which pioneered a model uniting bricks-and-mortar bookstores with the book club idea (see Section 3.1). Bertelsmann may have copied and expanded Foyle's idea or developed what it called the two-level method for itself.[219] With this model, Bertelsmann originally outsourced recruitment and membership management. Booksellers could also act as book club recruiters and entrepreneurs with a shop-in-shop model. Bertelsmann's unconventional recruitment methods, including door-to-door sales and circa 200 rolling bookshop buses sporting the Lesering logo, were notorious and often criticized.[220] The downside of the two-level method was the lack of control of the subcontractors. The method was enormously successful, with membership numbers skyrocketing from 200,000 after one and a half years to 1.6 million within six years. Staggering numbers such as these demanded significant investments and company restructuring. Bertelsmann transitioned into a holding company and the publisher C. Bertelsmann Verlag was separated from the Bertelsmann Lesering GmbH. Heavy investment in new forms of data management, such as early data processing machines and a punch card system, was undertaken and later replaced by data storage on magnetic tape in the 1960s.[221] This is also one reason why magazine publishers were often quite successful as book club operators across a variety of national markets: they had the knowhow and technology to handle large customer datasets for their high-circulation magazines.[222] For an indicator of the enormous amount of data and mail that was being handled, perhaps a picture of then-BOMC president Axel Rosin with 175,000 pieces of mail from members that had accumulated over a three-day weekend will suffice.[223] An excellent example of a successful transition from magazine

[219] Cf. Lokatis, pp. 135–45.

[220] Cf. ibid. and also "Die Bestsellerfabrik," pp. 32–41.

[221] Lokatis, "A Concept Circles the Globe," pp. 139–7.

[222] Cf. comment on US magazine publishers in Strout, "Book Club Publishing," p. 71.

[223] Cf. E. Havemann, "No More a Headache, Book Business Booms," *LIFE*, 50 (May 12, 1961), 19, 108–18, 118.

publisher into the mail-order business is the Scholastic Book Club (founded in 1948, still in existence today), which works through schools to deliver books to children and formed the basis for the trade publisher Scholastic – today the largest children's publisher in the world.[224]

The curation element within the four Cs usually meant selection and recommendation of content. Book clubs often published the recommendations as additional material in the magalogs or in small leaflets that accompanied the selected books. Both of these publication forms are epitexts in Genette's terminology. The additional material could be a summary of the book but more often contained an explanation of the choice by a judge or an editor of the club. The club members thus received more than just the original book. The 1950s, however, gave rise to a different form of curation that did not entail adding material, but rather extracting material. Strout maintains that "the decade's unique contribution to the book club idea" was the condensation of content into abridged editions or collected volumes of abbreviated texts.[225] The premier example of this type of club is the Reader's Digest Condensed Editions club (founded in 1950, re-named as Reader's Digest Select Editions in 1997, still in existence), which amassed 450,000 US subscribers within one year of its inception and had 2.2 million members by 1957. The book series brand was also extended to the UK and Australia from 1954 onward.[226] For purposes of comparison: at the same time, the two major US clubs working together as the US version of Book Club Associates (Doubleday), the Dollar Book Club and the Literary Guild, had approximately 400,000 and 800,000 members, respectively. The BOMC had about 500,000 members in 1957. The critical voices that had raised concerns about the preselection of books balked at the idea of abridgments. *The Nation* commented ironically that book clubs offered

---

[224] For more context, cf. R. Hogue Wojahn, "Book Clubs for Children in the United States," in J. Zipes (ed.), *The Oxford Encyclopedia of Children's Literature* (Oxford: Oxford University Press, 2006), www.oxfordreference.com/view/10 .1093/acref/9780195146561.001.0001/acref-9780195146561-e-0366.

[225] Strout, "Book Club Publishing," p. 75.

[226] Cf. British Library catalog. For more context, cf. E. Volkersz, "McBook: The Reader's Digest Condensed Books Franchise," *Publishing Research Quarterly*, 11 (1995), 2, 52–61.

"to save a potential reader the chore of reading all the reviews and making up his own mind,"[227] followed by a taunt of Reader's Digest Condensed Editions as "evaporated" texts.[228]

As discussed in Section 3.2, an impressive level of diversification of book clubs by target groups had already taken place before WWII. This diversification according to genres, demographics, and interest groups continued to play an important role, but a second type of diversification came onto the scene in the 1950s with different media becoming widely available – and easily transportable by mail. Record clubs sprung up in the postwar period.[229] While too broad in scope to cover in detail here, it is important to note that the big players in the book club business had started adding records to their portfolios by the mid-1950s. Later, clubs would add audio- and videocassettes as well as CDs and DVDs to their catalogs; the BOMC even owned a radio station briefly in the 1950s.[230] The Bertelsmann Lesering was flanked by the Schallplattenring from 1956 onward. Analogous to book clubs, the advertisements for the Schallplattenring immediately sold not only LPs but also a piece of furniture that offered a record player, a modern bar shelf, and storage for LPs.[231] A targeted expansion and merger strategy made Bertelsmann the market leader for music publishing in Germany by the 1970s.[232] Since – as Reinhard Mohn stated – "music, as a product, is much more interchangeable internationally" than print media,[233] the music business pioneered internationalization strategies within the Bertelsmann conglomerate that later applied to print publishing, especially book publishing, as well.

---

[227] D. Cort, "Culture Once a Month . . . The Book Clubs," *The Nation*, 184 (Feb. 16, 1957) 7, 133–6, 133.

[228] Ibid., 136.

[229] P. L. Miller, "Record Clubs. They Illustrate Trend in Selling Disks," *New York Times* (March 18, 1956), M3.

[230] Cf. "Book Club to Buy FM Station WABF," *New York Times* (June 18, 1954), 32.

[231] Cf. P. Wicke, "A Corporation Writes Music History," in *175 Years of Bertelsmann*, pp. 174–207, 175.

[232] Ibid., pp. 182–91.   [233] Ibid., p. 193.

By the end of the 1960s, the big players in the book club business had been established and were well aware of the different international market situations. The signs of the times pointed to expansion and diversification as well as consolidation. In Germany, both Bertelsmann and Holtzbrinck had a firm foothold in the mail-order market, and both clubs operated several hundred club shops in the pedestrian zones of German towns and cities. The club shops drew members and nonmembers alike, who could shop there, though only members would receive discounts. The shops thus anchored the club brands within the cityscape and offered an additional opportunity for member recruitment.

Overall, Bertelsmann in particular had practically reached its limits of growth within Germany, meaning that further growth strategies would explore the international realm. Bertelsmann's first step into international waters was in 1962, with the expansion into Spain. While the first book club had been established in Spain in 1930 modeled on the BOMC and similar curation enterprises,[234] Bertelsmann was involved in the 1962 foundation of Círculo de Lectores, modeled on the Bertelsmann Lesering. As the archival record shows, Bertelsmann representatives saw parallels between 1950s Germany and 1960s Spain: little to no book infrastructure and prior censorship conditions.[235] The expansion course was set and Bertelsmann soon entered the market in Austria (1966) and the Netherlands and Belgium (1967), followed by thirty-two other national markets until 2005 (Russia). Holtzbrinck expanded significantly within the German publishing industry and bought its way into important German publishing houses like S. Fischer and Rowohlt but also followed Bertelsmann into the international arena, collaborating with Swiss, Austrian, and Dutch companies in the late 1960s.[236] Especially in the 1960s, book industry members compared the aggressive expansion strategies with warmongering: "First the Germans

---

[234] Cf. F. Douglas, "Spain Now Has Its Book Club," *New York Times Book Review* (Aug. 3, 1930), 8–10.

[235] Cf. Lokatis, "A Concept Circles the Globe," p. 158.

[236] See also "Christ und Geld: Verleger/Holtzbrinck," *Spiegel*, 22 (March 18, 1968), 12, 174. See also "Nie Komplexe: Verlage," *Spiegel*, 25 (May 31, 1971), 23, 133.

came with their tanks in World War II, now here they come with their books."[237]

3.4 Mergers and Competition (1970s to 1990s)

By the 1970s and 1980s, some book clubs such as the Literary Guild, BOMC, and the Büchergilde Gutenberg were able to celebrate half a century of company history. Some traditional brands were present in multiple markets, such as the Literary Guild (Australia, Canada, UK, US). Other traditional players had folded, such as the British Book Society (1969). Book clubs were called a "sleepy business" and an "old literary institution"[238] by some, while others credited them with a "sudden rush in the 1970s to shake off the lethargy" of earlier decades.[239] The *Times*, similarly, saw British book clubs "once again flourishing" in 1979[240] after a "chapter of uncertainties" in the 1960s.[241] Al Silverman, CEO of the BOMC from 1972 to 1988, succinctly described the situation of book clubs, explaining that the book club business circled around a matrix of different considerations. The matrix he described was composed of three types of issues: (1) publishing and curation, (2) membership, and (3) competition.

Firstly, there were the traditional issues related to publishing and curation: "the books themselves; presentation of books; timing of books; pricing of books."[242] Interestingly, in the 1970s, book clubs popped up that played on the weaknesses of the big clubs and their inflexibility. For instance, the Book Find Club stated in ads that it could find "watershed works" and "unknowns," not needing to "play it safe"

---

[237] Quoted in Lokatis, "A Concept Circles the Globe," p. 154.

[238] Glaberson, "The Book Clubs, Chapter 2," p. 153.

[239] Weyr, "The Booming Book Clubs," p. 259.

[240] R. Berthoud, "In a tight situation . . . ?," *Times* (Dec. 19, 1979), 12.

[241] T. Barrett, "Book Clubs Faced with a Chapter of Uncertainties," *Times* (Dec. 25, 1966), 13.

[242] A. Silverman, "Book Clubs in America," in W. G. Graham and R. Abel (eds.), *The Book in the United States Today* (New Brunswick, NJ: Transaction, 1997), pp. 113–27, 118.

like the big clubs.[243] The big clubs needed to choose books that would appeal to a large membership, across a variety of tastes. According to Al Silverman, Main Selections were accepted by about 50 percent of the members after WWII, guaranteeing sales of about 400,000 copies of one title – a star-studded sales figure by any accounts. Over time, however, the "diminishing allure of the Main Selection" became a core challenge for the BOMC. Silverman shows that the acceptance rate declined rapidly after the 1950s: in 1962, it was at 26.8 percent; in 1972, 17.7 percent; in 1982, 13.5 percent; and by the mid-1990s, it had fallen "into single-digit figures."[244]

Secondly, Silverman delineated membership-related issues: "sociology of members and knowing about their wants and needs; serving the members." An important element of knowing members' wants and needs was keeping the acceptance rate high for the Main Selections to ensure high print runs and thus benefit from the economies of scale. Another element of membership-related issues was "recruiting new members." Here, Silverman emphasized, "the major clubs lose about 50% of their active members each year."

Finally and thirdly, he discussed the competition book clubs were facing "from the discount superstore chains" as well as "from the new and all-pervasive technology – CDs, CD-ROMs, video games, the Internet, all designed to steal more precious leisure time from reading."[245] The competition from the discount superstore chains, at least, was encroaching on the idea of convenience. Superstore chains eliminated Schwellenangst and offered customers convenience through their accessibility and ubiquity. Later, the convenience factor was supplemented by extra comfort through the inclusion of coffee bars in the superstores.

Most of Silverman's observations apply across all markets and decades – at least the first and second group of issues, and the third point, the competition, was particularly important in the 1970s and onward. Sources show, however,

---

[243] The Book Find Club, "In May of 1966, the number one bestseller … " [advertisement], *LIFE*, 70 (26 Mar 1971) 11, 52.

[244] Silverman, "Book Clubs in America," p. 119. [245] Ibid.

that the book club business was still alive and well in the 1970s and 1980s and still growing, albeit at a slower pace than in the 1950s and 1960s.[246]

In a 1970 article in Germany's weekly magazine *Der Spiegel*, a Bertelsmann CEO stated that recruitment had become so expensive that instead of recruiting new members, Bertelsmann had decided to buy up existing clubs – and thus gain members of those clubs – instead: "we don't have to recruit if we can buy."[247] A central step in international book club history was the expansion of Bertelsmann's book club business into the UK in 1977 and the United States in 1986 (takeover of Doubleday including book clubs in the United States, Canada, New Zealand, and Australia as well as a 50 percent in BCA[248]).

In 1977, Bertelsmann founded the Leisure Circle and introduced its tried-and-tested yet "controversial method of recruitment . . . concentrated on door-to-door canvassing" to the UK.[249] The Leisure Circle had "somewhat less than half a million"[250] members in 1984 and 350,000 in 1988, when it was merged with BCA.[251] Through the merger, Bertelsmann bought its way into BCA, which was a major player in book publishing as long as the Net Book Agreement was in place and there were only limited alternatives to the high street shops, that is, the downtown bookstores. Bertelsmann held onto its 50 percent share of BCA until 2008. Afterward, BCA was heavily restructured and eventually dissolved in 2013.[252] These mergers and acquisitions were major steps that paved the way for the fusion of Random House and Penguin in 2013, creating the biggest trade publisher in the world.

---

[246] For US numbers cf., e.g., L. J. Miller and D. P. Nord, "Reading the Data on Books, Newspapers, and Magazines. A Statistical Appendix," in D. P. Nord (ed.), *The Enduring Book. Print Culture in Post-War America* (Chapel Hill: University of North Carolina Press, 2009), pp. 503–18, 514.

[247] "Was wir kaufen können . . . brauchen wir nicht zu werben." See also "Kaufen können," p. 241.

[248] Cf. M&MC: *Book Club Associates and Leisure Circle*, p. 5.

[249] E. J. Craddock, "Clubbing Together," *Times* (Aug. 6, 1984), 6. [250] Ibid.

[251] Cf. M&MC: *Book Club Associates and Leisure Circle*, p. 9.

[252] L. Campbell, "BCA Parent Company Enters Administration," *The Bookseller* (March 6, 2012), www.thebookseller.com/news/bca-parent-company-enters-administration.

Holtzbrinck, though similar in its drive for expansion, followed a slightly different strategy, investing more in publishing houses on a national and international scale. By 1986, Holtzbrinck also had a significant foothold in the US publishing industry as owner of Bantam Books and Henry Holt.[253]

During the 1970s in Germany, an initiative formed that bore certain similarities to Gollancz' Left Book Club and was touted as a "most ambitious publishing project."[254] The Syndikat Buchgesellschaft für Wissenschaft und Literatur (founded in 1976, discontinued in the 1990s) planned to distribute left-wing, political, academic texts and was founded by leading intellectuals of the time, Axel Rütters and Karl Markus Michel, who both had worked for the prestigious Suhrkamp Verlag. The Syndikat concept was a particular combination of a collaboratively owned publishing house, funded by authors, and a book club. The book club guaranteed its members curation of and access to critical, economically risky texts that mainstream publishers would not or could not make available. The Syndikat also offered a sense of community and belonging by organizing annual discussion meetings to the participating authors and members. The Syndikat project had an intellectual profile, but its reach was smaller than that of the Left Book Club. The academic orientation of the program limited its potential readership: in 1992, at its peak, 10,600 members sourced their academic texts from Syndikat.[255] Nonetheless, its connectedness with historical precursors such as the Left Book Club and other left-wing book clubs of the 1920s and 1930s as well as its overlap with the 2015 crowdfunding-based relaunch of the Left Book Club remind us of the "constant, energetic interplay between people, places and things" that Shep's model highlights.[256]

Syndikat worked from the bottom up, and so did two entrepreneurs in the UK in the 1980s. Ted Smart and Seni Glaister created an alternative to

---

[253] Cf. J. Tagliabue, "Publisher Began with Book Club," *New York Times* (July 4, 1986), D3.

[254] "das ehrgeizigste verlegerische Unternehmen." R. Michaelis, "Neue Heimat für Kritik: "Syndikat": Wissenschaftsverlag, Buchgesellschaft, Forum," *Zeit* (March 12, 1976), 12, www.zeit.de/1976/12/neue-heimat-fuer-kritik/komplettansicht.

[255] Cf. Mainzer Verlagsarchiv, Syndikat, Syn 28.

[256] Shep, "Books in Global Perspectives," p. 66.

the book clubs, based on direct sales: Book People (founded in 1988, still in existence today). The Book People sell a small, curated selection of books by presenting them at workplaces, factories, and offices "to people who thought books weren't for them, people who never went into bookshops, people who had not opened a book since school."[257] With a convenient distribution model and curation, the Book People offer prospective readers books at a hefty discount but without any obligation. The Book People have had peak years with 14 million books distributed per annum through its drop-off system as well as through a mail-order catalog (started in 1995) and online bookstore. The Book People and similar efforts, such as the direct seller Kinderland in Germany (founded in 2000, still in existence today, specializing in children's books), offer benefits of book clubs without any membership obligation.

3.5 The Demise of Book Sales Clubs (from the 1990s to approximately 2010)

The 1990s brought about significant changes in the industry, on national and international levels. In the UK, the 1990s marked the end of the Net Book Agreement, which heavily impacted the sales of book clubs. The impact was immediate and had large-scale repercussions for the book club business in the UK. The history of the biggest British player Book Club Associates (BCA) is illustrative of this impact. BCA had been founded in 1966, and Bertelsmann had entered the British market by buying its way into BCA in 1977. For most of the 1980s, 50 percent of BCA belonged to Bertelsmann and 50 percent to W. H. Smith. As Eric de Bellaigue shows, when Reed bought 50 percent of BCA from Smith in 1988, the investment cost Reed 52 million GBP. Only ten years later, one year after the demise of the Net Book Agreement, 50 percent of BCA was sold off for "well under 40 million GBP."[258]

Globally, book industry concentration and consolidation were in full swing. The power in the market had clearly shifted toward the big

---

[257] S. Garfield, "The Book Marketeers," *The Guardian* (Aug. 4, 2002), www .theguardian.com/books/2002/aug/04/society.

[258] Cf. E. de Bellaigue, *British Book Publishing as a Business since the 1960s* (London: British Library, 2004), p. 127.

bookstore chains, which offered their customers concession and convenience. Community and curation were less pronounced here, but customer appreciation and loyalty programs nodded toward these two elements with personal shopping days, targeted advertising, specialized discounts, and more. These elaborate customer loyalty schemes also gave the booksellers access to the type of large-scale market research data that had hitherto only been available to institutions like book clubs.[259] In addition, in particular in the United States and the UK, supermarkets and mass-merchandising chains such as Costco, Sainsbury's, and Target became increasingly important as retail outlets, selling large quantities of best-sellers to people who may have accessed books through mail-order previously. The supermarkets "were retail venues that reached deep into the community." The supermarket book racks guaranteed accessibility to "certain kinds of books," far away from urban centers and at all hours of the day.[260] In Germany, newspapers – established media like *Zeit* or *Süddeutsche Zeitung*, but also yellow press like *Bild* – began offering popular and highly affordable editions of classics and newer titles to their readers from 2004 onward, essentially drawing potential members away from the clubs.[261] The *New York Times* wrote, "the era of blockbuster authors, ubiquitous book superstores and online retailers has not been kind to the book club."[262] The competition was indeed harsh. In a telling statement in 1991, then-president of the BOMC, James L. Mercer, said, "It's not enough to be a cultural service . . . We aim to get tough on marketing and merchandising, just as the chains have been."[263]

Cartoonist Randy Jones illustrated the *New York Times* article that quoted Mercer. His cartoon displayed salespeople dressing up the book club –

---

[259] Cf. Striphas, *The Late Age of Print*, pp. 184–5.

[260] Thompson, *Merchants of Culture*, pp. 47–8.

[261] Cf. J. Wilke, "Bücher (und andere Medien) als Zusatzgeschäfte von Zeitungs- und Zeitschriftenverlagen," *Gutenberg-Jahrbuch*, 82 (2007), 348–64.

[262] D. D. Kirkpatrick, "The Book-of-the-Month Club Tries to Be More Of-the-Moment," *New York Times* (June 28, 2001), E1–5, E1.

[263] R. Cohen, "As Rivals Grow, Book Clubs Dress Up Their Marketing," *New York Times* (March 11, 1991), D12.

depicted as a book with an old man's balding head – with new accessories and a toupee. The salespeople are using a dust jacket labeled "razzle dazzle" to freshen up the book club's old-fashioned style.[264] By the end of the millennium, razzle-dazzle was no longer sufficient to battle the competition. The 1990s had seen an ongoing slump in the mail-order segment, which hit Reader's Digest particularly hard. In an interesting move, Bookspan, a "gargantuan club," was created in March 2000 as a partnership – a virtual monopoly – between Doubleday Direct (DD), then owned by Bertelsmann, and BOMC, then owned by Time Warner.[265] With the merger, Bookspan accounted for more than "$900 million or 72% of the $1.3 billion book clubs market revenues" in the United States annually, with 10 million members and 3,000 employees.[266] Only a "smattering of small, independent book clubs" remained,[267] and one of the main goals was to "ultimately transform the institutions into a digital hybrid catering to dozens of narrow markets."[268] In 2001, Bookspan was trying out ten new clubs a year, "from erotica to gardening."[269] Bookspan also tried to diversify its income stream in 2006 by publishing original work.[270] All of these efforts, however, did not lead to the projected success, and Bertelsmann sold Bookspan to Najafi Companies in 2008. Since then, Bookspan has been sold to the rather enigmatic company Pride Tree Holdings (2012), where it remains to this day.[271] In one fell swoop, Bertelsmann sold its stake in North American, British, Australian, New Zealand, Dutch, Polish, Russian, Czech, and Ukrainian book clubs, disentangling the global direct mail book industry that had grown together over decades.[272] Citing this sale, the German trade magazine *Börsenblatt*

---

[264] R. Jones, "Book Club Razzle Dazzle" [Cartoon], *New York Times* (March 11, 1991), D12.

[265] Oda and Sanislo, *Book Publishing USA*, p. 35. [266] Ibid. [267] Ibid., p. 36.

[268] Carvajal, "Well-Known Book Clubs Agree to Form Partnership," C2.

[269] Kirkpatrick, "The Book-of-the-Month Club Tries to Be More Of-the-Moment," p. E5.

[270] J. Milliot, "Bookspan as Publisher," *Publishers Weekly* (April 7, 2006), www .publishersweekly.com/pw/print/20060410/4353-bookspan-as-publisher.html.

[271] For more detail, cf. Norrick-Rühl, "'Stimulating our Literature . . . ,'" p. 249–51.

[272] Cf. "Bertelsmann will weitere Buchclubs verkaufen," *Börsenblatt* (July 16, 2008), www.boersenblatt.net/220120.

warned, "memento mori, book clubs" in 2010, convinced that mail order's decline was unstoppable.[273] For Germany's big club, the end was indeed near: Bertelsmann closed its former cash cow Bertelsmann Club in 2015.[274] The importance of community and belonging became palpable after the closure was announced. Former Bertelsmann Club editors Sabine Pauli and Silvia Krysciak stated that for those approximately 1.5 million members who had remained loyal, the closure was a devastating blow. As the club closed, the remaining employees received feedback from members who had been in the club for decades, and their sense of loss was profound.[275]

4 Chances and Challenges for Book Clubs Today

As the second decade of the twenty-first century draws to a close, the term "book club" is more readily associated with celebrities such as Richard (Madeley) and Judy (Finnegan), Oprah Winfrey, and Reese Witherspoon than with the big popular book sales clubs. As James Atlas argued in the *New York Times*, the boom of book groups is rooted in a search for community. "In the end," Atlas writes, "book groups are about community. . . . We spend our days at airports or commuting to work; our children come and go; our friends climb up and down the social ladder; we change jobs and move house. No one knows their neighbor. But a lot of us are reading *The Goldfinch*."[276]

Book clubs are, admittedly, still in existence as a distribution channel, but the numbers show overwhelmingly that the traditional book club model is no longer a big market factor. The decline of book clubs in Germany, which we have seen has the longest-running history of book clubs, is clearly

---

[273] C. Weileder, "Buchgemeinschaften – memento mori?" *Börsenblatt* (July 8, 2010), www.boersenblatt.net/artikel-.389023.html.

[274] Cf., see also, "Bertelsmann sagt dem Club bye, bye," *Börsenblatt* (June 17, 2014), www.boersenblatt.net/artikel-ende_2015_ist_schluss.802943.html.

[275] Cf. Semi-structured interviews with S. Pauli, Berlin (March 27, 2019) and S. Krysciak, Berlin (March 28, 2019).

[276] J. Atlas, "Really? You're Not in a Book Club?" *New York Times* (March 22, 2014), www.nytimes.com/2014/03/23/opinion/sunday/really-youre-not-in-a-book-club.html.

visible in data from *Buch und Buchhandel in Zahlen* (see Figure 1) – the only growth indicated since 1976 was caused by a brief influx of members from the new Bundesländer after the German reunification in 1989.

A recent overview of the European marketplace showed book clubs were in steady decline from 2012 (4.7 percent of the European publishers' revenue) to 2016 (1.7 percent).[277] In the UK, the numbers for book clubs/direct sellers declined noticeably from 8 percent in 2009 to 3 percent in 2013.[278] According to BookNet Canada, only 2.7 percent of books in 2015 were purchased through book club memberships (although this number was up from 1.8 percent in 2013).[279] In Denmark, Finland, and Norway, according to statistics published by the respective national publisher associations, the numbers are still a bit higher, between 6 percent (Denmark)[280] and 8 percent (Finland)[281], for mail-order and club sales. A longitudinal study for Norway clearly visualizes the decline from 20 percent in 2007 to 7 percent in 2017.[282] After sales declined by 50 percent from 2012 to 2017, the largest French book club, France Loisirs (founded by Bertelsmann in 1970, sold to the French conglomerate Actissia in

---

[277] P. Anderson, "Trends in the European Marketplace: 2016 Numbers Stable, and Affected by Pound Sterling Slump," *Publishing Perspectives* (Jan. 10, 2018), https://publishingperspectives.com/2018/01/european-publishers-federation-statistics-2016/.

[278] The Booksellers Association of the UK and Ireland, "UK Book Sales. Source of Purchase 2009–2014" (2015), https://booksellers.org.uk/BookSellers/BizFormFiles/3432732c-4ae9-4173-bf21-38a48d1e32b8.pdf, p. 1.

[279] Cf. BookNetCanada, "Canada Sales Channel Book Purchase Share," *Statista* (2019) www.statista.com/statistics/470157/canada-sales-channel-book-purchase-share/.

[280] Cf. Boghandlerforeningen, "Survey on Place of Book Purchasing in Denmark," *Statista* (2019), www.statista.com/statistics/631489/survey-on-place-of-book-purchasing-in-denmark/.

[281] Cf. Kirjakauppaliitto, "Distribution of Print Book Sales in Finland in 2016, by Sales Channel," *Statista* (2019), www.statista.com/statistics/678080/finland-printed-book-sales-revenue-share-by-distribution-channel/.

[282] Cf. Den norske Bokhandlerforening, "Where Did You Buy Your Last Book?" *Statista* (2019), www.statista.com/statistics/744571/survey-on-location-of-recent-book-purchase-in-norway/.

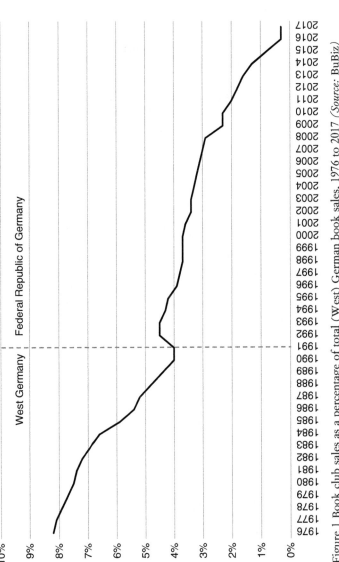

Figure 1 Book club sales as a percentage of total (West) German book sales, 1976 to 2017 *(Source:* BuBiz*)*

2011) declared bankruptcy in 2017. While a new investor was found, the investor announced in 2018 that 450 jobs would be cut.[283]

Repeatedly, the same reasons crop up: competition from online retailing and other media, decline of reading in society, decline of (physical) book ownership, lack of willingness to subscribe or be a member. Ironically, with the shift into e-commerce, we have seen an unexpected transition back into subscription models. It is no fluke that the book *Subscribed: Why the Subscription Model Will Be Your Company's Future—and What to Do About It* by Tien Tzuo and Gabe Weisert achieved best-seller status in 2018.

Do today's readers still seek convenience, curation, concession, and community? The answer is quite simple: yes. In fact, the employees and former employees of book clubs interviewed for this research agreed that readers still need all four of these elements.

Regarding convenience, however, Amazon has formed a monopoly that no other actor in the industry can compete with. Though the Kindle is, in effect, a type of limitation and subscription, consumers do not feel patronized by it and do not seem to understand that they have bought into a closed-circuit, proprietary system not so unlike a book club.[284]

The semi-structured interviews all confirmed that curation is key in an oversaturated market, but it is the market for attention that book clubs are competing in as well. With "quality TV" and original streaming series at our fingertips, it is easy to read less and enjoy other forms of storytelling instead. BookChoice, a Dutch start-up, claims that it is a "book club for the digital age" and offers monthly e-book choices and audiobooks to its members. A German subsidiary failed to catch on, but the Dutch start-up has been in business since 2014.[285] In Brazil, TAGLivros, founded in 2014,

[283] Cf. "France Loisirs will 450 Stellen streichen," *Börsenblatt* (April 3, 2018), www.boersenblatt.net/artikel-sparkurs_bei_franzoesischem_buchclub.1448802.html.

[284] Cf. Interview with S. Krysciak (March 28, 2019).

[285] Cf. S. van Endert, "Interview mit Bookchoice-Geschäftsführer Nathan Hull," *Börsenblatt* (Oct. 9, 2017), www.boersenblatt.net/artikel-interview_mit_book choice-geschaeftsfuehrer_nathan_hull.1384349.html.

offers curation with an annual or monthly subscription model but also emphasizes the sense of community building with online and offline meetings of members to discuss books. The club has managed to reach 37,000 members within a four-year period.[286] In 2018, a US initiative called Spread the Words, essentially an e-book club, was announced in partnership with an existing web community, The FabOverFifty. Spread the Words also highlights the importance of community through virtual discussions with authors and other readers.[287]

Independent publishers have also embraced subscription models, expertly combining them with aspects of crowdfunding to secure their position in a highly concentrated marketplace. Two interesting examples from Great Britain are the Pound Project, which combines the goal of supporting authors sustainably with an idealistic approach to reading.[288] The not-for-profit publisher And Other Stories, known for its focus on translations in a marketplace traditionally hostile to translated fiction, works with a flat rate subscription model to help fund its book projects and has found its niche with a recognizable design and translations from under-represented language communities.[289]

Two of the interviews were conducted with employees of long-standing German book clubs, Büchergilde Gutenberg and Wissenschaftliche Buchgesellschaft (WBG, established in 1949). Both the Büchergilde and the WBG have found their own ways of persevering into the twenty-first century. Both clubs offer their members curated content and discounts within a market that is otherwise defined by fixed book prices. They also

---

[286] P. Anderson, "At Frankfurt's 'The Markets' Conference: Brazil's Gustavo Lembert," *Publishing Perspectives* (Oct. 2, 2018), https://publishingperspectives.com/2018/10/frankfurter-buchmesse-the-markets-conference-2018-brazil-gustavo-lembert/.

[287] P. Anderson, "Open Road Launches New Book Club with Fab Over Fifty," *Publishing Perspectives* (Sept. 10, 2018), https://publishingperspectives.com/2018/09/industry-notes-open-road-book-club-partnership-fab-over-fifty/.

[288] Cf. M. Flatt, "The Pound Project Wants to Make Reading Accessible to All," *The Bookseller* (Sept. 17, 2018), www.thebookseller.com/futurebook/pound-project-847736.

[289] Cf. S. Tobler, "And Other Stories," *Logos*, 24 (2013), 4, 7–11.

both heavily emphasize the element of community. The Wissenschaftliche Buchgesellschaft is essentially a nonprofit publisher whose current 85,000 members finance the publishing activities with an annual membership fee and thus have access to concessions on the books they buy. It is geared to an academic audience, with textbooks, text editions, and so on particularly for scholars and students in the humanities and social sciences. WBG has been focusing increasingly on members' benefits such as exclusive event access, discussion groups, or discounts on general admission to museums all over Germany – a new position, that of a "community manager" has recently been created.[290] The WBG's character as a niche club, building on an existing academic community and drawing new members from incoming students and early career researchers, may prove to be the key to survival.

As previously mentioned, the Büchergilde relies heavily on its status as a book club for book lovers and bibliophiles – as did the Folio Society, which no longer acts as a book club in the traditional sense. Special peritexts for members – a particular choice of paper and the overall book design, cover, and interior illustration – are a membership benefit. This can be seen as part of the curation process: the goal is not only to select the must-have texts but also to create an attractive and exclusive book that the members will want to read, own, and present. Simultaneously, the edition can be sold at a lower price when compared with the trade edition: interesting book design at a reliable discount. This combination may be the key to surviving for the Büchergilde: "as a book's materiality becomes in a sense optional, it will only grow in significance, seen more than ever as a manifestation of cultural expression and meaning."[291] And in the age of Instagram and bookstagramming, the idea of special editions, visibly set apart from the mainstream, may offer an opportunity for marketing and communications.[292] As members of book clubs

---

[290] Cf. semi-structured interview with Götz Fuchs (Feb. 13, 2019).

[291] M. Benton, "Books," in S. Wajda and H. Sheumaker (eds.), *Material Culture in America. Understanding Everyday Life* (Santa Barbara, CA: ABC-CLIO, 2007), pp. 70–4, 74.

[292] Cf. H. Connolly, "Is Social Media Influencing Book Cover Design?" *The Guardian* (Aug. 28, 2018), www.theguardian.com/books/2018/aug/28/is-social-media-influencing-book-cover-design.

today, readers can be subscribers as indicated by Ray Murray and Squires in their updated communications circuit, but they can also be content generators; readers can be subscribers – and crowdfunders, a fact that the Büchergilde recently drew upon to secure its independence. In 2014, for its ninetieth birthday, the Büchergilde shifted to an incorporated collective model. In the first four years, 1,090 readers joined the Büchergilde as associates. Associates buy a minimum of one share for 500 € and can hold a maximum of 100 shares. This company structure makes the community idea very visible. Natalie Acksteiner, currently public relations representative of the Büchergilde, emphasized that associates and members alike shared a strong connection to book culture.[293] The Büchergilde will soon be a century old; despite moments in its more recent history where massive restructuring was necessary and dissolution was imminent, the outlook today seems promising. In 2018, the Büchergilde had 60,000 members in Germany and 2,300 in Switzerland, and the new members recruited recently have been younger readers, "closer to 30 than 50."[294]

Bookspan today still has eight clubs to its name – and the BOMC. The BOMC – a brand almost as old as the Büchergilde brand – has chosen a different pathway to persevere in the current book industry. It was relaunched by Bookspan as a subscription box service under the hipper name Book of the Month – BOTM – in 2016 to reshape its brand for a new generation of readers. The BOTM recommends five new books – sometimes before they appear elsewhere – and members can either choose one (or more) per month or skip the month entirely.[295] In 2016, this was a radical move for the traditional brand, but by that time, *Publishers Weekly* already considered subscription boxes "big business."[296] In *Publishing Research Quarterly*, Neil Goff wrote in 2011, "direct-marketing

---

[293] Cf. semi-structured interview with N. Acksteiner (Feb. 5, 2019).

[294] K. Mühleck, "'Die Mühen der Ebenen': Interview mit Alexander Elspas," *Börsenblatt* (July 9, 2018), www.boersenblatt.net/artikel-interview_mit_alexander_elspas.1490190.html.

[295] Cf. Norrick-Rühl, "Stimulating Our Literature," pp. 250–1.

[296] J. McCartney, "How One Bestselling Indie Author Became a Book Box Entrepreneur," *Publishers Weekly* (Feb. 19, 2016), www.publishersweekly.com

skills sets have changed very little" – it is the context that has. As Goff says, "The 'snail mail' box has given way to the email box and social media sites."[297] Today, subscription book boxes are firmly established in everyday book culture. The website mysubscriptionaddiction.com lists available subscription box services for Canada, the UK, New Zealand, and the United States. In 2018 and 2019, the numbers have been rather consistent with between 137 and 140 book box subscriptions available continuously,[298] ranging from Stars Hollow Book Club for Gilmore Girl fans to the more mainstream Owlcrate for YA literature. The American Marketing Association has been monitoring the subscription box trend and explains, "Consumers are flinging open their doors and welcoming brands into their lives through the subscri[p]tion box model. ... Consumers' willingness to roll out the welcome mat ... – and cough up quite a bit of data – stems from the trendy desire for a bespoke customer experience. ... They want a curated collection of products without stepping foot in a store."[299] A recent study for the US consumer market shows that subscription box users are likely to be younger millennials (18 to 24 years of age), majority female, have a college degree or are students and live in college towns or "hipster enclaves."[300] They are also more likely than other consumers to pay attention to online reviews and post reviews online themselves; they consider themselves to be interested in the arts to a higher degree than average consumers. Rachel Noorda recently analyzed the success of US subscription boxes, focusing on the element of "curated surprise" in subscription boxes.[301] She also discussed

/pw/by-topic/authors/pw-select/article/69455-how-one-bestselling-indie-author-became-a-book-box-entrepreneur.html.

[297] N. Goff, "Direct-Response Bookselling," *Publishing Research Quarterly*, 27 (2011), 3, 259–67, 267.

[298] July 2018: 137 boxes; January 2019: 139 boxes; April 2019: 140 boxes.

[299] S. Steimer, "Marketers Use Subscription Boxes Strategically," *American Marketing Association* (Jan. 1, 2018), www.ama.org/marketing-news/marketers-use-subscription-boxes-strategically/.

[300] Cf. Hitwise, "Subscription Boxes in 2018" (April 2018), http://hitwise.connexity.com/rs/371-PLE-119/images/Subscription-Box-Report-2018.pdf, p. 7.

[301] Noorda, "The Element of Surprise," p. 234.

the popularity of box subscriptions as gifts. This combines two elements of our model: convenience for the gift buyer and curation for the gift receiver.

Convenience and curation are the most important selling points for subscription book boxes, though concession also plays a role: "There's something so gratifying about finding a package at your door after a long, hard day of work. Even though you may have ordered it yourself, it feels akin to a gift – opening and unwrapping whatever's inside."[302] For the element of community, readers turn to social media: "Subscription boxes satisfy this appetite for a detached yet customized shopper experience, and they do so with the climactic bonus of unboxing." Consumers "want to showcase it all on social media, sometimes for fans they've never met."[303] Bookstagram offers endless possibilities for book box subscribers, and the BOTM, for instance, heavily encourages postings.

Obviously, not every former book sales club has a future as a subscription book box service. Bookspan decision makers clearly saw potential in the long-standing BOMC brand and thus moved it into the digital literary sphere. A recent infographic details the prominent role of a Book of the Month choice in creating book buzz, citing the example of Celeste Ng's *Little Fires Everywhere*, which was one of the five books presented to members of the BOTM in September 2017.[304] Here, we can see that book club choices today still can contribute to the success and status of a book. Interestingly, the BOTM has been focusing on debut novels recently, which can have a positive effect for the entire industry. For instance, in the four-month period from January to April 2019, 45 percent

[302] C. DesMarais, "Here's How Much People Like Their Subscription Boxes (Infographic)," *Inc.com* (Aug. 8, 2016), www.inc.com/christina-desmarais/heres-data-showing-the-crazy-growth-of-subscription-box-services-infographic.html.

[303] Steimer, "Marketers Use Subscription Boxes."

[304] P. Anderson, "At BookExpo, Penguin and Goodreads Chart the Blaze of Celeste Ng's 'Little Fires Everywhere,'" *Publishing Perspectives* (June 1, 2018), https://publishingperspectives.com/2018/06/goodreads-penguin-random-house-book expo-celeste-ng-2018/.

of the choices were debut novels. In the one-year period from May 2018 to April 2019, 32 percent were debut novels.[305]

For the digital literary sphere, Murray identifies the following five categories: performing authorship, "selling" literature, curating the public life of literature, consecrating the literary, and entering literary discussion. All of these categories were fulfilled by the book clubs in the twentieth century – and many of these categories apply to the book clubs that remain active today. In particular, Murray's last category is of interest regarding the creation of a sense of community and belonging among members.

Another common denominator – and perhaps even a fifth C for book clubs in the twenty-first century? – of the Wissenschaftliche Buchgesellschaft, Buechergilde, and the Book of the Month subscription box service is commitment to the field. All three award prizes to support their values and either consecrate the literary, as Murray writes, or elevate book culture in a wider sense. Starting in 2019, the WBG will annually award a prize for a nonfiction book – members are eligible to nominate books themselves.[306] The Büchergilde has awarded a design prize for young illustrators since 2002 and founded a literacy campaign in 2011.[307] The BOTM awards an annual prize for the best book of the year, including members in voting: the Lolly – named for the first-ever BOMC book, *Lolly Willowes* by Sylvia Townsend Warner.[308] These prizes generate media attention and strengthen the book club brands and also reinforce the sense of community for their members.

---

[305] Cf. BOTM, "Past Months" (2019), www.bookofthemonth.com/add-ons/past-months.

[306] Wissenschaftliche Buchgesellschaft, "Wissen! Der Sachbuchpreis der WBG für Geisteswissenschaften" [2018], www.wbg-wissen-preis.de/Home/Jury.

[307] Büchergilde Gutenberg, "Von der Buchgemeinschaft zur Kulturgemeinschaft" (2019), www.buechergilde.de/id-2000er-jahre.html.

[308] BOTM, "Introducing the Lolly" (Dec. 9, 2016), www.bookofthemonth.com/blog/introducing-the-lolly-191.

5 Conclusions and Outlook

This Element started with cartoons and will end with one. There are dozens to choose from. At least in the United States, cartoons joking about book clubs are a constant concomitant of book club history. Garfield, Ziggy, Peanuts, and Marmaduke – classic and favorite cartoon characters – have debated the merits and pitfalls of monthly subscription services. The large selection of cartoons dealing with book clubs, in particular with the Book-of-the-Month brand, underlines how firmly subscription models are embedded in the cultural memory of readers.

"I never noticed how quickly time passes until I joined a Book of the Month Club," says a woman, sitting on the couch next to her partner.[309] Her apartment is overflowing with books. The books have reached couch level, and they cover her knees; a book covers her partner's head while he drinks coffee. But she is reading and seems unfazed by the avalanche of books surrounding her. Why is this a good choice for a closing cartoon? Because it visualizes, albeit in a tough-in-cheek way, the millions of books that reached readers through mail-order distribution.

We have seen in this Element that book clubs and book commerce are linked inextricably, and that our book industry today was shaped by and through activities by book clubs, and by "people, places and things," as Sydney Shep describes.[310] The people who contribute to book club history are authors, too, but more centrally, they are book club founders and innovators, judges, editors, managers. The places that define book club history can be better described as nodes in a global network, forged through emigration and immigration at the beginning of the twentieth century, but also by mergers across and beyond national boundaries, channels, and oceans. Finally, the things that shape book club history are the book club editions, the books themselves, and their paratexts: magalogs, brochures, advertisements. Millions of books reached millions of readers as book club

---

[309] J. Deering, "I never noticed how quickly . . . , " in *Strange Brew* (Feb. 15, 2016), archived in *CartoonistGroup*, www.cartoonistgroup.com/store/add.php? iid=139258.

[310] Shep, "Books in global perspectives," p. 66.

editions. These editions, though rather uninteresting to collectors today, were objects of desire, of identification and pride. Millions of pages of colorful, highly readable book-related content entered households through the mail: mail-order book culture at its most effective. The loss of this high-circulation book advertising has been linked to the recent massive dip in readers in Germany.[311] However, as Donald Strout wrote, it is "far harder to weigh" the impact of book clubs than to count the "cumulative millions" of readers reached and books and catalogs mailed throughout book club history.[312]

Throughout, this minigraph has argued that a global perspective is necessary to understand the cultural and economic impact of book clubs as a distribution channel in the twentieth and into the twenty-first centuries. While the horizon of this Element did not allow the perspective to be broadened beyond Germany, the UK, and the United States, future research can profit from the application of Shep's model to book club history. Further, we have seen that the central reasons for membership in clubs can be condensed into four succinct categories: convenience, community, concession, and most importantly curation. Within McCleery's metaphor, these similarities across national boundaries and the decades are the traces in the palimpsest, still visible today in conglomerate structures and a handful of resilient book clubs but also resurfacing in new, innovative ways.

This Element has also shown, I hope, the enormous potential that further research into book club history offers. There is much work to be done to update and internationalize the existing research. We can work together to compare and contrast book club choices across national contexts to understand how book clubs contributed to the flow of translation and the proliferation of mass culture in the international realm. When we declutter shelves and stumble upon old book club editions, we can rediscover books

---

[311] Cf. a comment by S. Bublitz, quotrf in M. Roesler-Graichen, "Am Ende der Lesekultur? Podium Die Zukunft des Buchmarkts," *Börsenblatt* (Dec. 12, 2017), www.boersenblatt.net/artikel-
podium__die_zukunft_des_buchmarkts_.1410990.html.

[312] Strout, "Book Club Publishing," 79.

that were enormously popular in the twentieth century but have been all but erased from the canon today.

As Amaranth Borsuk concludes in her treatise on the book, "While reading on digital devices is not going away, one technology clearly does not supersede the other."[313] Similarly, I would argue, one distribution channel does not supersede the other. We have briefly nodded toward the book discussion club boom of the late twentieth century, and its new surge in recent years on social media. Where and when the distribution model meets the discussion group, whether online or in person, there is still potential for the distribution model. As we have briefly seen, where and when commitment to literature and society come together with the objectives and mission of niche book clubs, there is still potential for growth. Book historians and industry experts alike will be watching closely.

[313] A. Borsuk, *The Book* (Cambridge, MA: MIT Press, 2018), p. 258.

Bibliography

Websites

ABAA: Glossary of Terms. www.abaa.org/glossary/entry/book-club-edition

And Other Stories. www.andotherstories.org/

Börsenverein des deutschen Buchhandels: Preisbindungsrechtliche Kriterien für Buchgemeischaftsausgaben. www.boersenverein.de/beratung-service/abc-des-zwischenbuchhandels/details/potsdamer-protokoll/.

Book-of-the-Month (BOTM). www.bookofthemonth.com/

BOTM (2016) "Introducing the Lolly" (9 Dec.), www.bookofthemonth.com/blog/introducing-the-lolly-191

BOTM. (2019) "Past months," www.bookofthemonth.com/add-ons/past-months

Bookspan. http://bookspan.com/

British Library Catalogue. http://explore.bl.uk

Büchergilde Gutenberg. www.buechergilde.de

Büchergilde Gutenberg. (2019) "Prämierte Bücher." www.buechergilde.de/praemierte-buecher.html

Büchergilde Gutenberg, "Von der Buchgemeinschaft zur Kulturgemeinschaft" (2019), www.buechergilde.de/id-2000er-jahre.html

Deutsche Nationalbibliothek Catalogue. https://portal.dnb.de/opac.htm

Facebook Page of the Quality Paperback Book Club. www.facebook.com/QPBBookClub/

Folio Society. www.foliosociety.com/

Hitwise (2018) Subscription Boxes in 2018. US Market, http://hitwise.connexity.com/rs/371-PLE-119/images/Subscription-Box-Report-2018.pdf

Immerwahr, D. The Books of the Century. www.booksofthecentury.com [lists all BOMC selections from 1926 to 1974]

Left Book Club. www.leftbookclub.com/

Library of Congress Catalog. https://catalog.loc.gov/

My Subscription Addiction. www.mysubscriptionaddiction.com/

Pound Project. www.poundproject.co.uk/about

Quality Paperback Book Club. www.qpb.com

Steimer, S. (2018), American Marketing Association: Marketers Use Subscription Boxes Strategically. www.ama.org/marketing-news/ marketers-use-subscription-boxes-strategically/

Urban Dictionary. (2008), 2Good: Unboxing. www.urbandictionary.com/ define.php?term=unboxing

VGV Kinderland. www.kinderland.de

Wilson, N. The Book Society Site: About. https://thebooksocietysite .com/about/

Wissenschaftliche Buchgesellschaft. www.wbg-wissenverbindet.de/

Wissenschaftliche Buchgesellschaft, "Wissen! Der Sachbuchpreis der WBG für Geisteswissenschaften" [2018], www.wbg-wissen-preis.de /Home/Jury.

Yourdictionary.com. Schwellenangst. www.yourdictionary.com/ schwellenangst.

Sources and References

Adams, T. & Barker, N. (2006) A New Model for the Study of the Book. In D. Finkelstein & A. McCleery, eds, *The Book History Reader*, 2nd edn, Abingdon: Routledge, pp. 47–65.

Adorno, T. W. (2003) Résumé über Kulturindustrie. In R. Tiedemann & T. W. Adorno, eds, *Gesammelte Schriften*, Frankfurt/Main: Suhrkamp, pp. 337–45.

Anderson, P. (2018) At BookExpo, Penguin and Goodreads Chart the Blaze of Celeste Ng's "Little Fires Everywhere". *Publishing Perspectives* (June 1), https://publishingperspectives.com/2018/06/goodreads-penguin-random-house-bookexpo-celeste-ng–2018/.

(2018) At Frankfurt's The Markets" Conference: Brazil's Gustavo Lembert. *Publishing Perspectives* (Oct. 2), https://publishingperspectives.com/2018/10/frankfurter-buchmesse-the-markets-conference-2018-brazil-gustavo-lembert/.

(2018) Open Road Launches New Book Club With Fab Over Fifty. *Publishing Perspectives* (Sept. 10), https://publishingperspectives.com/2018/09/industry-notes-open-road-book-club-partnership-fab-over-fifty/.

(2018) Trends in the European Marketplace: 2016 Numbers Stable, and Affected by Pound Sterling Slump. *Publishing Perspectives* (Jan. 10), https://publishingperspectives.com/2018/01/european-publishers-federation-statistics–2016/.

Appelbaum, J. (1982) Paperback Talk. Sales Through the Mails. *New York Times Book Review* (Nov. 28), 31–2.

Arnold, M. (2001) Making Books. Book Clubs With a Mission. *New York Times* (Jan. 11), www.nytimes.com/2001/01/11/books/making-books-book-clubs-with-a-mission.html.

Atlas, J. (2014) Really? You're Not in a Book Club? *New York Times* (Mar. 22), www.nytimes.com/2014/03/23/opinion/sunday/really-youre-not-in-a-book-club.html.

Baker, J. (1957) Book Clubs. In J. Hampden, ed., *The Book World today: A New Survey of the Making and Distribution of Books in Britain*, London: Allen & Unwin, pp. 120–7.

Barrett, J. H. et al. (1955) Postal Charges for Books [letter to the editor]. *Times* (Dec. 8), 11.

Barrett, T. (1966) Book Clubs Faced with a Chapter of Uncertainties. *Times* (Dec. 25), 13.

Barzun, J. (2001) Foreword: Three Men and a Book. In A. Krystal, ed., *A Company of Readers: Uncollected Writings of W.H. Auden, Jacques Barzun, and Lionel Trilling from the Readers' Subscription and Mid-Century Book Clubs*, New York: Free Press, pp. ix–xvii.

Benton, M. (2007) Books. In S. Wajda & H. Sheumaker (eds), *Material Culture in America. Understanding Everyday Life*, Santa Barbara, CA: ABC-CLIO, pp. 70–4.

Berger, S. E. (2016) *The Dictionary of the Book. A Glossary for Book Collectors, Booksellers, Librarians, and Others*, Lanham: Rowman & Littlefield.

Berthoud, R. (1979) In a Tight Situation Will the Book Business Break Out of Its Hard Times? *Times* (Dec. 19), 12.

Bhaskar, M. (2016) *Curation. The Power of Selection in a World of Excess*, London: Piatkus.

Boghandlerforeningen. (2019) Survey on Place of Book Purchasing in Denmark. *Statista*, www.statista.com/statistics/631489/survey-on-place-of-book-purchasing-in-denmark/.

Bonner, D. (2008) *Revolutionizing Children's Records. The Young People's Records and Children's Record Guild Series, 1946–1977*, Lanham: Scarecrow Press.

The Book Find Club. (1971) In May of 1966, the number one bestseller . . . [advertisement]. *LIFE*, 70 (Mar. 26) 11, 52.

BookNetCanada. (2019) Canada Sales Channel Book Purchase Share. *Statista*, www.statista.com/statistics/470157/canada-sales-channel-book-purchase-share/.

Book-of-the-Month Club. (1946) Beautiful Library Sets [advertisement]. *LIFE*, 21 (Nov. 25) 22, 3.

(1960) Your choice of valuable library sets [advertisement]. *LIFE*, 49 (Nov. 14) 20, 8–9.

(1979) Give us your friends . . . [advertisement, ID code C274]. Owned by author.

The Booksellers Association of the UK and Ireland (2015). UK Book Sales. Source of Purchase 2009–2014. https://booksellers.org.uk/BookSellers/ BizFormFiles/3432732 c-4ae9-4173-bf21-38a48d1e32b8.pdf.

Book Society. (1955) "this way . . . there's always time for a book" [advertisement]. *Times* (Sept. 23), 10.

Borsuk, A. (2018) *The Book*, Cambridge, MA: The MIT Press.

Bourdieu, P. (1999) *Die Regeln der Kunst. Genese und Struktur des litera-rischen Feldes*, Frankfurt/Main: Suhrkamp.

Campbell, L. (2012) BCA Parent Company Enters Administration. *The Bookseller* (6 Mar.), www.thebookseller.com/news/bca-parent-company-enters-administration.

Carter, D. (2015) Middlebrow Book Culture. In M. Savage & L. Hanquinet, eds., *Routledge International Handbook of the Sociology of Art and Culture*, New York: Routledge, pp. 349–69.

Carvajal, D. (2000) Well-Known Book Clubs Agree to Form Partnership. *New York Times* (March 2), C2.

Clark, G. & Phillips, A. (2014) *Inside Book Publishing*, 5th edn, Abingdon: Routledge.

The Classics Club. (1943) Free as a Trial-membership Gift from The Classics Club [advertisement]. *LIFE*, 15 (Nov. 8) 19, 5.

Cohen, R. (1991) As Rivals Grow, Book Clubs Dress Up Their Marketing. *New York Times* (March 11), D12.

Connolly, H. (2018) Is Social Media Influencing Book Cover Design? *The Guardian* (28 Aug.), www.theguardian.com/books/2018/aug/28/is-social-media-influencing-book-cover-design.

Coopey, R., O' Connell, S. & Porter, D. (1999) Mail Order in the United Kingdom c. 1880–1960: How Mail Order Competed with Other

Forms of Retailing. *The International Review of Retail. Distribution and Consumer Research*, 3, 261–73.

Cort, D. (1957) Culture Once a Month … The Book Clubs. *The Nation*, 184 (Feb. 16) 7, 133–6.

Covington, H. (2006) *Literary Divas: The Top 100+ Most Admired African-American Women in Literature*, Phoenix, AZ: Amber.

Craddock, E. J. (1984) Clubbing together. *Times* (Aug. 6), 6.

(1985) Signs of Success. *Times* (May 27), 7.

Daniels, H. (2002) *Literature Circle: Voice and Choice in Book Clubs and Reading Groups*, 2nd edn. Portsmouth, NH: Stenhouse Publishers.

Darnton, R. (1982) What Is the History of Books? *Daedalus*, 111 (3) 3, 65–83.

Davis, K. C. (1984) *Two-Bit Culture: The Paperbacking of America*, Boston: Houghton Mifflin.

de Bellaigue, E. (2004) *British Book Publishing as a Business since the 1960s*, London: British Library.

DesMarais, C. (2016) Here's How Much People Like Their Subscription Boxes (Infographic). *Inc.com* (Aug. 8), www.inc.com/christina-desmarais/heres-data-showing-the-crazy-growth-of-subscription-box-services-infographic.html.

Dittmar, H. (1991) Meanings of Material Possessions as Reflections of Identity: Gender and Social-Material Position in Society. *Journal of Social Behavior and Personality*, 6 (6), 165–86

DMA. (2019) Number of Catalogs Mailed in the United States from 2001 to 2015 (in billions). *Statista*, www.statista.com/statistics/735150/catalogs-mailed-usa/.

Douglas, F. (1930) Spain Now Has Its Book Club. *New York Times Book Review* (Aug. 3), pp. 8–10.

Doyle, T. (2003) Collecting the Science Fiction Book Club. *BookThink. Resources for Booksellers* (Nov. 3), www.bookthink.com/0005/05sfb.htm.

Dumont, V. (2017) Literatur- und Buchvermittlung an ein Millionenpublikum. Charakteristika der Literatur- und Buchdiskurse in den Mitgliederzeitschriften der Büchergilde Gutenberg und des Bertelsmann-Leserings in den 1950er Jahren. *Gutenberg-Jahrbuch*, 92, 181–200.

Enzensberger, H. M. (1964) Bildung als Konsumgut: Analyse der Taschenbuch-Produktion. In H. M. Enzensberger, ed., *Bewußtseins-Industrie*, Frankfurt/Main: Suhrkamp, pp. 134–66.

Estermann, M. (2013) Buchhandel, Buchhandelsgeschichte und Verlagsgeschichtsschreibung vom 18. Jahrhundert bis zur Gegenwart. In U. Rautenberg, ed., *Buchwissenschaft in Deutschland*, Berlin/Boston: de Gruyter Saur, pp. 257–320.

Evans, M. D. R., Kelley, J., & Sikora, J. (2014) Scholarly Culture and Academic Performance in 42 Nations. *Social Forces*, 92 (4), 1573–1605. https://doi.org/10.1093/sf/sou030.

Farr, C. K. (2004) *Reading Oprah: How Oprah's Book Club Changed the Way America Reads*, Albany: State University of New York Press.

Findlay, B. (2010) Subscription publishing. In M. F. Suarez & S. J. & H. R. Woodhuysen, eds., *Oxford Companion to the Book*, Oxford: Oxford University Press, vol. 2, pp. 1186–7.

Fitzgerald, E. (1985) *A Nickel an Inch. A Memoir*, New York: Atheneum.

Flatt, M. (2018) The Pound Project Wants to Make Reading Accessible to All. *The Bookseller* (Sept. 17), www.thebookseller.com/futurebook/pound-project–847736.

Flood, A. (2016) Left Book Club Bids to Crowdfund Radical Reading, with Help of Chomsky. *The Guardian* (Oct. 20), www.theguardian.com/books/2016/oct/20/left-book-club-crowdfund-radical-reading-network.

Foyle, W. A. (1937) The New Writer [letter to the editor]. *Times* (Oct. 5), 10.

Franklin, A. (2018) The Profits from Publishing: A Publisher's Perspective. *The Bookseller* (March 2), www.thebookseller.com/blogs/profits-publishing-publishers-perspective–743231#

Füssel, S. (2010) The Bertelsmann Book Publishing Companies. 1945 to 2010. In *175 Years of Bertelsmann. The Legacy for our Future*, Gütersloh: Bertelsmann, pp. 86–129.

Garfield, S. (2002) The Book Marketeers. *The Guardian* (Aug. 4), www.theguardian.com/books/2002/aug/04/society.

Gastell, D. (2012) Verlagsgeschichtsschreibung ohne Verlagsarchiv. In C. Norrick & U. Schneider, eds., *Verlagsgeschichtsschreibung. Modelle und Archivfunde*, Wiesbaden: Harrassowitz, pp. 46–59.

Genette, G. (1997) *Paratexts. Thresholds of Interpretation*, Cambridge: Cambridge University Press.

Gilbert, E. D. (2010) Mail-order Catalog. In M. F. Suarez & S. J. & H. R. Woodhuysen, eds., *Oxford Companion to the Book*, Oxford: Oxford University Press, vol. 2, pp. 907–8.

Glaberson, W. (1987) The Book Clubs, Chapter 2. *New York Times* (July 12), 153.

Glaister, G. A. (1996) *Encyclopedia of the Book*, 2nd edn., New Castle, DE: Oak Knoll Press.

Goff, N. (2011) Direct-Response Bookselling. How It Died, Why It Is Alive Again, and Why It Will Become Even More Important in the Future. *Publishing Research Quarterly*, 27 (3), 259–67.

Hackenberg, M. (2005) The Subscription Publishing Network in Nineteenth-Century America. In M. Hackenberg, ed., *Getting the Books Out. Papers of the Chicago Conference on the Book in 19th-Century America*, Honolulu: University Press of the Pacific, pp. 45–75.

Harker, J. (2007) *America the Middlebrow. Women's Novels, Progressivism, and Middlebrow Authorship between the Wars*. Amherst/Boston: University of Massachusetts Press.

Harvey, R. C. (2013). Helen E. Hokinson. *The Comics Journal* (July 22), www.tcj.com/helen-e-hokinson/.

Haugland, A. (2000) Book Propaganda: Edward L. Bernays's 1930 Campaign Against Dollar Books. *Book History*, 3, 231–52.

Havemann, E. (1961) No More a Headache, Book Business Booms. *LIFE*, 50 (May 12) 19, 108–18.

Henze, E. (1987) Buchgemeinschaften. In S. Corsten, S. Füssel, & G. Pflug, eds., *Lexikon des gesamten Buchwesens (LGB²)*, 2nd edn., Stuttgart: Hiersemann, vol. I: A–Buch, pp. 592–7.

Hogue Wojahn, R. (2006) Book Clubs for Children in the United States. In J. Zipes, ed., *The Oxford Encyclopedia of Children's Literature*, Oxford: Oxford University Press, www.oxfordreference.com/view/10.1093/acref/9780195146561.001.0001/acref-9780195146561-e-0366.

Hokinson, H. E. (1943) I'm afraid this is goodbye [Cartoon]. *New Yorker*, XIX (Nov. 13) 39, 105.

(1944) What I like about the Book-of-the-Month Club is the suspense [Cartoon]. *New Yorker*, XX (July 29) 24, 57.

Holtmann, J. P. (2008) *Pfadabhängigkeit strategischer Entscheidungen. Eine Fallstudie am Beispiel des Bertelsmann Buchclubs Deutschland.* Cologne: Kölner Wissenschaftsverlag.

Hopf, C. (2010) Qualitative Interviews – ein Überblick. In U. Flick et al., eds., *Qualitative Forschung. Ein Handbuch*, 8th edn., Reinbek: Rowohlt, pp. 349–60.

Howsam, L. (2015) Book History in the Classroom. In L. Howsam, ed., *The Cambridge Companion to the History of the Book*, Cambridge: Cambridge University Press, pp. 253–67.

Howsam, L. (2006) *Old Books and New Histories. An Orientation to Studies in Book and Print Culture*, Toronto/Buffalo/London: University of Toronto Press.

Hutchens, J. K. (1946) For Better or Worse, the Book Clubs. Their Organization, Aires, Methods and the Mass Market They Have Created. *New York Times Book Review* (March 31), 1, 24–8.

Hutter, M. & Langenbucher, W. R. (1980) *Buchgemeinschaften und Lesekultur: Studie zum Programmangebot von sechs Buchgemeinschaften (1972–1977)*, Berlin: Spiess.

Jones, R. (1991) Book Club Razzle Dazzle [Cartoon]. *New York Times* (March 11), D12.

Kappel, J. W. (1948) Book Clubs and Evaluations of Books. *Public Opinion Quarterly*, 12 (2), 243–52.

Kirjakauppaliitto. (2019) Distribution of Print Book Sales in Finland in 2016, by Sales Channel. *Statista*, www.statista.com/statistics/678080/fin land-printed-book-sales-revenue-share-by-distribution-channel/.

Kirkpatrick, D. D. (2001) The Book-of-the-Month Club Tries to Be More Of-the-Moment. *New York Times* (June 28), E1–5.

Klingenberg, J. (2019) *De Burger-Leeskring*: a Brief History of South Africa's First Commercial Book Club and its Effect on Afrikaans Literature. *Quaerendo* 49 (2), 158–179, https://doi.org/10.1163/15700690-12341440.

Kollmannsberger, M. (1995) *Buchgemeinschaften im deutschen Buchmarkt: Funktionen, Leistungen, Wechselwirkungen*, Wiesbaden: Harrassowitz.

Kuhn, A. (2012) Überlegungen zu einer systemtheoretischen Perspektive des Kulturbegriffs in der Verlagshistoriographie. In C. Norrick & U. Schneider, eds., *Verlagsgeschichtsschreibung. Modelle und Archivfunde*, Wiesbaden: Harrassowitz, pp. 113–35.

Lash, S. & Lury, C. (2007) *Global Culture Industry*, Cambridge: Polity.

Law, J., ed. (2016) *A Dictionary of Business and Management*, 6th edn., Oxford: Oxford University Press, www.oxfordreference.com/view/10.1093/acref/9780199684984.001.0001/acref-9780199684984-e-3873#.

Leavis, Q. D. (1979) *Fiction and the Reading Public*, Harmondsmouth: Penguin.

Bibliography

Lee, C. (1958) *The Hidden Public: The Story of the Book-of-the-Month Club*, New York: Doubleday.

Lokatis, S. (2010) A Concept Circles the Globe. From the Lesering to the Internationalization of the Club Business. In *175 Years of Bertelsmann. The Legacy for our Future*, Gütersloh: Bertelsmann, pp. 132–71.

Long, E. (2003) *Book Clubs: Women and the Uses of Reading in Everyday Life*, Chicago: University of Chicago Press.

Macauley, T. (1930) Book Club Debate Again On in England. *New York Times* (March 9), E3.

MacDonald, D. (1952) The Book-of-the-Millennium Club. *New Yorker*, XXVIII (Nov. 29) 41, 171–88.

Marsden, S. (2018) "I Didn't Know You Could Read." Questioning the Legitimacy of Kim Kardashian-West's Status as a Cultural and Literary Intermediary. *Logos*, 29 (2–3), 64–79. https://doi.org/10.1163/18784712-02902008.

McCartney, J. (2016) How One Bestselling Indie Author Became a Book Box Entrepreneur. *Publishers Weekly* (Feb. 19), www.publishersweekly.com/pw/by-topic/authors/pw-select/article/69455-how-one-bestsellingindie-author-became-a-book-box-entrepreneur.html.

McCleery, A. (2015) The Book in the Long Twentieth Century. In L. Howsam, ed., *The Cambridge Companion to the History of the Book*, Cambridge: Cambridge University Press, pp. 162–80.

Meier, B. (1981) Leseverhalten unter soziokulturellem Aspekt. *Archiv für Soziologie und Wirtschaftsfragen des Buchhandels* (March 27) LI, W1327–407; (Aug. 21) LII, W1411–98; (Sept. 1) LIII, W1503–86.

Menand, L. (2011) Browbeaten. Dwight Macdonald's War on Midcult. *New Yorker*, LXXXVII (Sept. 5) 26, 72–8.

Michaelis, R. (1976) Neue Heimat für Kritik: "Syndikat": Wissenschaftsverlag, Buchgesellschaft, Forum. *Zeit* (March 12) 12, www.zeit.de/1976/12/neue-heimat-fuer-kritik/komplettansicht.

Miller, L. J. & Nord, D. P. (2009) Reading the Data on Books, Newspapers, and Magazines. A Statistical Appendix. In D. P. Nord, ed., *The Enduring Book. Print Culture in Post-War America*. Chapel Hill: University of North Carolina Press, pp. 503–18.

Miller, P. L. (1956) Record Clubs. They Illustrate Trend In Selling Disks. *New York Times* (March 18), M3.

Mitgang, H. (1978) Head of Book-of-Month Club to Retire Next Month. *New York Times* (Dec. 28), C16.

Monopolies and Mergers Commission: Book Club Associates and Leisure Circle. A Report on the Merger Situation, London: HM Stationery Office, 1988.

Mühleck, K. (2018) "Die Mühen der Ebenen": Interview mit Alexander Elspas. *Börsenblatt* (July 9), www.boersenblatt.net/artikel-interview_mit_alexander_elspas.1490190.html.

Murray, S. (2015) Charting the Digital Literary Sphere. *Contemporary Literature*, 56 (2), 311–39.

Nawotka, E. (2014) How the UK's Folio Society Is Changing with the Times. *Publishing Perspectives* (July 21), https://publishingperspectives.com/2014/07/how-the-uks-folio-society-is-changing-with-the-times/.

Niewiarra, M. & Gehrau, E. (1989) Buchgemeinschaften und Wettbewerb. In P. Vodosek, ed., *Das Buch in Praxis und Wissenschaft. 40 Jahre Deutsches Bucharchiv München*, Wiesbaden: Harrassowitz, pp. 263–94.

Noorda, R. (2019) The Element of Surprise: A Study of Children's Book Subscription Boxes in the USA. *Publishing Research Quarterly*, 35 (2), 223–34, https://doi.org/10.1007/s12109-019-09641-z.

Norrick-Rühl, C. (2017) Stimulating Our Literature and Deepening Our Culture. *Quaerendo*, 47 (3–4), 222–51, http://dx.doi.org/10.1163/15700690-12341383.

(2018) Two Peas in a Pod: Book Sales Clubs and Book Ownership in the Twentieth Century. In E. Stead, ed., *Reading Books and Prints as Cultural Objects*, Cham, Switzerland: Springer, pp. 231–50.

Den norske Bokhandlerforening. (2019) Where Did You Buy Your Last Book? *Statista*, www.statista.com/statistics/744571/survey-on-location-of-recent-book-purchase-in-norway/.

Oda, S. & Sanislo, G. (2001) *Book Publishing USA – Facts, Figures, Trends*, London: Holger Ehling.

Owen, L. (2006) *Selling Rights*, 5th edn., Abingdon: Routledge.

Pearce, S. (1995) *On Collecting. An Investigation into Collecting in the European Tradition*, London: Routledge.

Pyne, L. (2016) *Bookshelf*, New York: Bloomsbury Academic.

Radway, J. (1997) *A Feeling for Books. The Book-of-the-Month Club, Literary Taste, and Middle-Class Desire*, Chapel Hill: University of North Carolina Press.

Rainey, S. (1971) The Folio Society: Handsome Books at Minimal Cost. *The Courier*, 8 (3), 35–45.

Rautenberg, U., ed. (2015) *Reclams Sachlexikon des Buches*, Stuttgart: Reclam.

Ray Murray, P. & Squires, C. (2013) The Digital Publishing Communications Circuit. *Book 2.0*, 3 (1), 3–23.

Riberette, P. (1956) Les Clubs du Livre. *Bulletin des Bibliothèques de France* (6), 425–35, http://bbf.enssib.fr/consulter/bbf-1956-06-0425-003.

Rodgers, T. (2003) The Right Book Club: Text Wars, Modernity and Cultural Politics in the Late Thirties." *Literature & History*, 12 (2), 1–15, https://doi.org/10.7227/LH.12.2.1.

Roesler-Graichen, M. (2017) Am Ende der Lesekultur? Podium Die Zukunft des Buchmarkts. *Börsenblatt* (Dec. 12), www.boersenblatt.net/artikel-podium__die_zukunft_des_buchmarkts_.1410990.html.

Roscoe, J. (2018) "The Age of Shouting Had Arrived" Victor Gollancz, Stanley Morison, and the Reimagining of Marketing at Victor

Gollancz, Ltd and the Left Book Club. *Logos*, 29 (2–3), 9–25, https://doi.org/10.1163/18784712-02902003.

Rubin, J. S. (2004) The Book-of-the-Month Club. In P. S. Boyer, ed., *The Oxford Companion to United States History*, Oxford: Oxford UP, www.oxfordreference.com/view/10.1093/acref/9780195082098.001.0001/acref-9780195082098-e-0191.

   (1992) *The Making of Middlebrow Culture*, Chapel Hill, NC & London: University of North Carolina Press.

   (2018) Middlebrows. In I. Takayoshi, ed., *American Literature in Transition, 1920–1930*, Cambridge: Cambridge University Press, pp. 43–60.

Selwyn, P. (2000) *Everyday Life in the German Book Trade*, University Park: Pennsylvania State University Press.

Shatzkin, L. (1983) *In Cold Type: Overcoming the Book Crisis*, Boston: Houghton Mifflin.

Shep, S. (2015) Books in Global Perspectives. In L. Howsam, ed., *The Cambridge Companion to the History of the Book*, Cambridge: Cambridge University Press, pp. 53–70.

Sikora, J., Evans, M. D. R., & Kelley, J. (2019) Scholarly Culture: How Books in Adolescence Enhance Adult Literacy, Numeracy and Technology Skills in 31 Societies. *Social Science Research*, 77, 1–15, https://doi.org/10.1016/j.ssresearch.2018.10.003.

Silverman, A. (1997) Book Clubs in America. In W. G. Graham & R. Abel, eds., *The Book in the United States Today*, New Brunswick, NJ: Transaction, pp. 113–27.

S.a. (1968) Christ und Geld: Verleger / Holtzbrinck. *Der Spiegel*, 22 (18 Mar) 12, 174.

S.a. (2014) Bertelsmann sagt dem Club bye, bye. *Börsenblatt* (17 June), https://www.boersenblatt.net/artikel-ende_2015_ist_schluss.802943.html.

S.a. (2008) Bertelsmann will weitere Buchclubs verkaufen. *Börsenblatt* (16 July), https://www.boersenblatt.net/220120.

S.a. (1957) Boekenkasten voor Slagzinnen! *Nieuws* (Jan) 107, 3–5.

S.a. (1957) Boekenkasten voor Slagzinnen. *Nieuws* (Feb) 108, 7.

S.a. (1954) Book Club to Buy FM Station WABF. *The New York Times* (18 June), 32.

S.a. (1957) Die Bestsellerfabrik. Bertelsmann-Konzern. *Der Spiegel*, 11 (24 July) 30, 32–41.

S.a. (1953) Een oud-engels boekenkastje cadeau. *Nieuws* (Jan–Feb) 68, 6–7.

S.a. (2018) France Loisirs will 450 Stellen streichen. *Börsenblatt* (3 Apr), https://www.boersenblatt.net/artikel-sparkurs_bei_franzoe sischem_buchclub.1448802.html

S.a. (1973) Gute Nase. *Der Spiegel*, 27 (22 Oct) 43, 99–104.

S.a. (1970) Kaufen können: Verlage / Fusionen. *Der Spiegel*, 24 (27 Apr) 18, 241.

S.a. (1928) Literature for Youths. A Children's Book-of-the-Month Club to Be Organized. *The New York Times* (1 Nov), 23.

S.a. (1971) Nie Komplexe: Verlage. *Der Spiegel*, 25 (31 May) 23, 133.

S.a. (1929) Retailers Attack Book Club System. *The New York Times* (14 May), 25.

S.a. (1928) Start Catholic Book Club. *The New York Times* (23 April), 18.

S.a. (1941) Trainees Will Get Book Club Service. *The New York Times* (1 June), 39.

S.a. (1929) Two New Book Clubs for Children Merge. *The New York Times* (6 Aug), 26.

Solberg, J. L. (1999) Book Clubs. In R. Herbert, ed., *The Oxford Companion to Crime and Mystery Writing*, Oxford: Oxford University Press, pp. 43–4.

Stark, C. (2008) How to Identify Book Club Editions. *BookThink. Resources for Booksellers* (Nov. 6), www.bookthink.com/0005/05bce.htm.

Stern, M. B. (2005) Dissemination of Popular Books in the Midwest and Far West during the Nineteenth Century. In M. Hackenberg, ed., *Getting the Books Out. Papers of the Chicago Conference on the Book in 19th-Century America*, Honolulu: University Press of the Pacific, pp. 76–97.

Stevenson, I. (2010) *Book Makers. British Publishing in the Twentieth Century*, London: British Library.

Stringer, J., ed. (1996) *The Oxford Companion to Twentieth-Century Literature in English*, Oxford: Oxford University Press.

Striphas, T. (2009) *The Late Age of Print. Everyday Book Culture from Consumerism to Control*, New York: Columbia University Press.

Strout, D. E. (1958) Book Club Publishing. *Library Trends*, 7 (1), 66–81.

Sutherland, S. (2016) The Folio Society Is Ending Their Membership Program. *Alcuin Society Blog* (Aug. 19), http://alcuinsociety.com/folio-society-ending-their-membership-program/.

Tagliabue, J. (1986) Publisher Began with Book Club. *New York Times* (July 4), D3.

Thompson, J. B. (2012) *Merchants of Culture. The Publishing Business in the Twenty-First Century*, 2nd edn., New York: Plume.

Tobler, S. (2013) And Other Stories. *Logos*, 24 (4), 7–11, https://doi.org/10.1163/1878-4712-11112027.

Travis, T. (2002) Print and the Creation of Middlebrow Culture. In S. E. Casper, J. D. Chaison, & J. D. Groves, eds., *Perspectives on American Book History. Artifacts and Commentary*, Amherst: University of Massachusetts Press, pp. 339–66.

Universal Book Club (1939) Philipp Gibbs ... Join now – editions are limited [advertisement]. *Times* (Dec. 1), 4.

van Endert, S. (2017) Interview mit Bookchoice-Geschäftsführer Nathan Hull. *Börsenblatt* (Oct. 9), www.boersenblatt.net/artikel-interview_mit_bookchoice-geschaeftsfuehrer_nathan_hull.1384349.html.

van Melis, U. (2012) Buchgemeinschaften. In E. Fischer & S. Füssel, eds., *Geschichte des deutschen Buchhandels im 19. und 20. Jahrhundert. Band 2: Weimarer Republik. Teil 2*, Berlin: De Gruyter, pp. 553–88.

Volkersz, E. (1995) McBook: The Reader's Digest Condensed Books Franchise. *Publishing Research Quarterly*, 11 (2) 2, 52–61.

Volpers, H. (2002) Der internationale Buchmarkt. In J.-F. Leonhard et al., eds., *Medienwissenschaft: Ein Handbuch zur Entwicklung der Medien und Kommunikationsformen*, 3. Teilband, Berlin/New York: de Gruyter, pp. 2649–60.

Weileder, C. (2010) Buchgemeinschaften – memento mori? *Börsenblatt* (July 8), www.boersenblatt.net/artikel-.389023.html.

Weissbach, F. (1969) Buchgemeinschaften als Vertriebsform im Buchhandel. In *Buchgemeinschaften in Deutschland*, Hamburg: Verlag für Buchmarkt-Forschung, pp. 17–101.

Werner, M. & Zimmermann, B. (2006) Beyond Comparison: Histoire Croisée and the Challenge of Reflexivity. *History and Theory*, 45 (1) 1, 30–50.

West III, J. L. W. (2009) The Expansion of the National Book Trade System. In C. F. Kaestle & J. A. Radway, eds., *Print in Motion: The Expansion of Publishing and Reading in the United States, 1880–1940*, Chapel Hill: University of North Carolina Press, pp. 78–89.

Weyr, T. (1976) The Booming Book Clubs. In *The Business of Publishing*, New York: Bowker, pp. 259–85.

Whipple, L. (1929) Books on the Belt. *The Nation*, vol. 128, no. 3319, 182–3.

Wicke, P. (2010) A Corporation Writes Music History. In *175 Years of Bertelsmann. The Legacy for our Future*, Gütersloh: Bertelsmann, pp. 174–207.

Wilke, J. (2007) Bücher (und andere Medien) als Zusatzgeschäfte von Zeitungs- und Zeitschriftenverlagen. *Gutenberg-Jahrbuch*, 82, 348–64.

Wilson, M. R. (2004) Mail Order. In J. R. Grossmann, ed., *The Encyclopedia of Chicago*, Chicago: University of Chicago Press, pp. 505–6.

Wilson, N. (2017) Broadbrows and Book Clubs. *British Academy Review*, 29, 44–6.

(2018) Middlemen, Middlebrow, Broadbrow. In C. Ferrall & D. McNeill, eds., *British Literature in Transition, 1920–1940: Futility and Anarchy*, Cambridge: Cambridge University Press, pp. 315–30.

(2012) Virginia Woolf, Hugh Walpole, the Hogarth Press, and the Book Society. *English Literary History*, 79 (1), 237–60.

Winship, M. (2009) The Rise of a National Book Trade System in the United States. In C. F. Kaestle & J. A. Radway, eds., *Print in Motion: The Expansion of Publishing and Reading in the United States, 1880–1940*, Chapel Hill: University of North Carolina Press, pp. 56–77.

WIPO/IPA. (2018) *The Global Publishing Industry in 2016* [Geneva], www .wipo.int/edocs/pubdocs/en/wipo_ipa_pilotsurvey_2016.pdf.

Woodham, J. M., ed. (2016) *A Dictionary of Modern Design*, Oxford: Oxford University Press, www.oxfordreference.com/view/10.1093/acref/ 9780191762963.001.0001/acref-9780191762963-e-521.

World Books. (1939) T. E. Lawrence's masterpiece ... [advertisement]. *Times* (Dec. 12), 4.

Unpublished and Archival Materials

Bibliotheek van de Universiteit van Amsterdam

–   Nederlandse Boekenclub (1938–87) Bedrijfsdocumentatie Nederlandse Boekenclub – Den Haag, OTM: KVB PPA 366:5–367:7.
–   Nederlandse Boekenclub (1948–57) *Nieuws*, UBM: KVB t 624.
–   Siebenga, H. [1987] *Boekenclub en boekhandel; wedijverende verkoopkanalen*, Tilburg: Katholieke Universiteit Brabant, UBM: KVB VG 99:156.

Book-of-the-Month Club [1927] *An outline of a unique plan for those who wish to keep abreast of the best books of the day* [brochure], New York: BOMC. Digital copy, owned by author.

Deering, J. (2016) I never noticed how quickly . . . In *Strange Brew* (Feb. 15), archived in CartoonistGroup, www.cartoonistgroup.com/store/add.php?iid=139258.

Interviews

- with N. Acksteiner (PR representative of the Büchergilde Gutenberg), Frankfurt/Main (Feb. 5, 2019).
- with G. Fuchs (Community Manager of the Wissenschaftliche Buchgesellschaft), Darmstadt (Feb. 13, 2019).
- with S. Pauli (former employee of Bertelsmann Club), Berlin (March 27, 2019).
- with S. Krysciak (former employee of Bertelsmann Club and Büchergilde Gutenberg), Berlin (March 28, 2019).

Mainzer Verlagsarchiv Syndikat, Syn 28.

Schulz, C. (1971) Beagle Book Club. In *Peanuts* (April 8), archived in GoComics, www.gocomics.com/peanuts/1971/04/08.

Acknowledgments

Whether minigraphs or monographs: texts of any size, shape, and form develop over time. They come into being during slow phases of reading and fast bursts of writing, during and after conversations over coffee and conferences, and most importantly, within a network of scholarship, friendship, and support. I am grateful for the contributions of others that have made this Element a reality. There are too many to name all of them individually. In particular, I would like to thank:

Eben Muse, Samantha Rayner, and Bex Lyons and the team at Cambridge University Press for the opportunity to publish in this exciting new format;

the anonymous reviewers for their feedback;

the (former) book club employees who were willing to share their insights with me: Natalie Acksteiner, Götz Fuchs, Silvia Krysciak, and Sabine Pauli – and Silvia especially for her hospitality in Berlin;

Scarlett Saurat for her valuable editorial assistance and transcription of the interviews;

Neal R. Norrick for comments on drafts;

the archivists and librarians who facilitated access to materials and books at a number of institutions, including but not limited to the library of the Universiteit van Amsterdam and the Mainzer Verlagsarchiv;

and colleagues at conferences in Freiburg (2015), Paris (SHARP 2016), Parramatta (SHARP 2018), and Amherst (SHARP 2019), where I gave papers that fed into this research.

For a unique combination of friendship and scholarship, I am grateful to Dr. Melanie Ramdarshan Bold, Dr. Tobias Boll, and Dr. Anke Vogel.

For book talk and beyond in this busy phase of my life, I thank Marcella Behrens, Taryn Dynok Handt, and Dr. Karoline F. Kraft.

Timo Rühl contributes implicitly and immeasurably to all that I do, while Anton and Charlotte Rühl wreak havoc in my bookshelves and distract me from writing. Of all the reasons we academics have for missing deadlines, my children are my favorite.

In closing, I would especially like to thank Petra Norrick. Her grandparenting style is no less than supercalifragilisticexpialidocious, and if it weren't for her (often spontaneous and always generous) support, this Element would certainly still be an incomplete file on my computer. I dedicate this book to my mother as a small token of my appreciation.

Cambridge Elements ☰

Publishing and Book Culture

SERIES EDITOR

Samantha Rayner
University College London

Samantha Rayner is a Reader in UCL's Department of Information Studies. She is also Director of UCL's Centre for Publishing, co-Director of the Bloomsbury CHAPTER (Communication History, Authorship, Publishing, Textual Editing and Reading) and co-editor of the Academic Book of the Future BOOC (Book as Open Online Content) with UCL Press.

ASSOCIATE EDITOR

Rebecca Lyons
University of Bristol

Rebecca Lyons is a Teaching Fellow at the University of Bristol. She is also co-editor of the experimental BOOC (Book as Open Online Content) at UCL Press. She teaches and researches book and reading history, particularly female owners and readers of Arthurian literature in fifteenth- and sixteenth-century England, and also has research interests in digital academic publishing.

ABOUT THE SERIES

This series aims to fill the demand for easily accessible, quality texts available for teaching and research in the diverse and dynamic fields of Publishing and Book Culture. Rigorously researched and peer-reviewed Elements will be published under themes, or "Gatherings." These Elements should be the first check point for researchers or students working on that area of publishing and book trade history and practice: we hope that, situated so logically at Cambridge University Press, where academic publishing in the UK began, it will develop to create an unrivalled space where these histories and practices can be investigated and preserved.

Cambridge Elements ⹅

Publishing and Book Culture

Bookshops and Bookselling

Gathering Editor: Eben Muse
Eben Muse is Senior Lecturer in Digital Media at Bangor University
and co-Director of the Stephen Colclough Centre for the History and
Culture of the Book. He studies the impact of digital technologies on
the cultural and commercial space of bookselling, and he is part-
owner of a used bookstore in the United States.

ELEMENTS IN THE GATHERING

Digital Authorship: Publishing in the Attention Economy
Lyle Skains

Capital Letters: The Economics of Academic Bookselling
J. M. Hawker

Book Clubs and Book Commerce
Corinna Norrick-Rühl

A full series listing is available at: www.cambridge.org/EPBC

CPSIA information can be obtained
at www.ICGtesting.com
Printed in the USA
LVHW051936040220
645828LV00020B/862